God bless you as you
continue to move for—

Angela R. Jones

MOVING FORWARD:
FINDING PURPOSE IN YOUR PAIN

Angela Roberts Jones
Foreword by Bishop Joseph Warren Walker, III

WESTBOW
PRESS®
A DIVISION OF THOMAS NELSON
& ZONDERVAN

Copyright © 2016 Angela Roberts Jones.

All rights reserved. No part of this book may be used or reproduced by any means, graphic, electronic, or mechanical, including photocopying, recording, taping or by any information storage retrieval system without the written permission of the author except in the case of brief quotations embodied in critical articles and reviews.

This book is a work of non-fiction. Unless otherwise noted, the author and the publisher make no explicit guarantees as to the accuracy of the information contained in this book and in some cases, names of people and places have been altered to protect their privacy.

WestBow Press books may be ordered through booksellers or by contacting:

WestBow Press
A Division of Thomas Nelson & Zondervan
1663 Liberty Drive
Bloomington, IN 47403
www.westbowpress.com
1 (866) 928-1240

Because of the dynamic nature of the Internet, any web addresses or links contained in this book may have changed since publication and may no longer be valid. The views expressed in this work are solely those of the author and do not necessarily reflect the views of the publisher, and the publisher hereby disclaims any responsibility for them.

Scripture taken from the New King James Version. Copyright © 1979, 1980, 1982 by Thomas Nelson, Inc. Used by permission. All rights reserved.

Scripture quotations taken from the Holy Bible, New Living Translation, Copyright © 1996, 2004. Used by permission of Tyndale House Publishers, Inc., Wheaton, Illinois 60189. All rights reserved.

New Life Version © Christian Literature International. Christian Literature International (CLI) is a non-profit ministry dedicated to publishing and providing the Word of God in a form that can be read and understood by new readers and the well-educated alike... and at an affordable price. We invite you to learn how the NEW LIFE Version unlocks the treasures of God's Word!

Any people depicted in stock imagery provided by Thinkstock are models, and such images are being used for illustrative purposes only. Certain stock imagery © Thinkstock.

ISBN: 978-1-5127-2958-0 (sc)
ISBN: 978-1-5127-2959-7 (hc)
ISBN: 978-1-5127-2957-3 (e)

Library of Congress Control Number: 2016901730

Print information available on the last page.

WestBow Press rev. date: 2/17/2016

*This book is dedicated in loving memory of my deceased spouse
Pastor Raliegh Anthony Jones, Sr.
June 16, 1954 – June 8, 2008*

Special acknowledgements and thanks to my children Jeremy and Jessica, and my step-son Raliegh, Jr. & his wife Marguerita, and grandchildren Amirah-Imani, Cassidy and Raliegh, III! We have struggled, cried, laughed and prayed together as God blessed us to pick up the pieces and move forward.

I am grateful for my mother and father, Rev. & Mrs. Beaufort & Geraldine Roberts who laid the foundation for my success in life, as well as my brother Marcus (Carol), and my sister Marcella (Boisy) and my deceased brother, Beaufort, Jr. (Butch). They have stood by us through it all. But mostly, apart from my relationship with God, our bond as a family has given me so much strength.

I appreciate and love my in-laws, Mr. & Mrs. Harold & Betty Jones (now deceased), and Donna (Herald), Bryant (Sharon) & Kenny (Janice). Thank God for the love, peace and unity we share.

And lastly, thank God for the Greenhill Church Family. Many wondered if we would make it. But through the power of the Holy Spirit, the love of God, and the Grace of the Lord Jesus Christ, we have been kept and empowered to move forward to continue to reach the world for Christ!

PRAISE GOD FROM WHOM ALL BLESSINGS FLOW!!

CONTENTS

Introduction... xi

SECTION ONE...... THE GRIEF STAGE

1. The Story.. 1
   Till Death Do Us Part
2. What Next......................................11
   Trust God Through The Process

SECTION TWO...... THE HEALING PROCESS BEGINS

3. Make an Adjustment............................. 23
   Trust God's Master Plan
4. Keep It Moving................................. 35
   In Spite of the Pain
5. Glance Back- Gaze Forward...................... 47
   Your Present Pain Will Not Paralyze Your Future

SECTION THREE...... THE STRENGTHENING PHASE

6. The Shift.......................................61
   From Marriage to Singleness
7. A New Beginning................................ 71
   Letting Go of the Old
8. Mourning or Happiness.......................... 89
   You Choose

FOREWORD

There are books I've read that I believe are essential and necessary for our journey of development. This is one of them. My friend Pastor Angela Jones has courageously tackled a tough issue and provided us all immeasurable insight. As a Pastor, I've often seen people struggle with bouncing back from painful situations and shift into a new dimension of purpose and destiny. The bridge between the two has often been long, but Pastor Jones shortens the distance by providing practical and profound principles.

It is a fact that the God's hopes for His people are chronicled in Isaiah 61, yet many are unable to realize it because of the un-reconciled issues in our lives. You cannot fix what you are not willing to face. This book challenges us to confront deep wounds in our past and charts a course for healing and wholeness. When we are whole, our relationships get better and ultimately our communities. If we don't deal with the critical issue of our pain and its impact on our lives, we run the risk of pushing people away God sends to help us.

God has an amazing purpose for you. There are chapters to be lived after traumatizing situations. In order to realize our purpose, we must be willing to shift. It's not a sprint, but it's a marathon. It's a process. This book begins that process one brick at a time. It is not for the faint at heart. This book is for those who refuse to be defined by their past and are willing to embrace a new future free from assumptions, and erroneous perceptions about everything and everybody. If you are willing to take this journey, do so with great expectancy. If you are ready to shift from your pain into your purpose, you will not be disappointed. This is a masterpiece.

Bishop Joseph Warren Walker, III
Senior Pastor Mt. Zion B. C. Nashville, TN
Presiding Bishop Full Gospel Baptist
Church Fellowship International

INTRODUCTION

Have you ever asked the question, "How do I move forward from here?" Many people have experienced horrific pain and desire to move forward. But reclaiming your life after the painful event of losing a loved one can be easier said than done. If you can relate in any way to losing a loved one, this book is for you. It chronicles my journey through the very painful but purposeful season of losing my spouse to the stages of overcoming grief and enjoying life. My motivation for writing this book can be summed up in the following scripture:

> All praise to God, the Father of our Lord Jesus Christ. God is our merciful Father and the source of all comfort. He comforts us in all our troubles so that we can comfort others. When they are troubled, we will be able to give them the same comfort God has given us. Even when we are weighed down with troubles, it is for your comfort and salvation! For when we ourselves are comforted, we will certainly comfort you. Then you can patiently endure the same things we suffer. 2 Corinthians 1: 3-4, 6 (NLT)

God led me through this journey of healing and poured into my soul his infinite power, peace and comfort. The same comfort, strength, and encouragement I received from God has inspired me to impart the same to others. I am sure that you will identify with some of the stages of grief and healing as you read my story, the principles, illustrations, and directives. My journey through this season of my life gave me great revelation on the faithfulness of God. In addition to personal testimonies, this book also offers valuable lessons that will provide insight and guidance on how to work through the pain and live a wholesome life with contentment and enjoyment. Therefore, this book is not just about grief, but it is about life. Grief and pain are just pieces that help to make the big picture of life.

Through this journey, I learned first that moving forward is slightly different from moving on. Compare this concept to the illustration of marching infantry soldiers. The drill Sergeant shouts the command, "Forward, March," and not "March, Forward." There is a difference. In other words, the command is first to look forward, think forward, then move or march forward. I equate moving on to living from day to day, from event to event driven by the strong desire to survive. On the other hand, I relate moving forward to living out God's purpose with deep determination and passion in spite of the challenges of grief. One can see the rainbow at the end of the storm when moving forward. There is something to reach for, to live for and yes, even to die for when moving forward.

Moving forward requires deep healing and the power and courage to adjust to a new life. It means that one moves beyond this point in life and away from the pain to peace, prosperity, new relationships, and elevation in personal development and contentment. The person who learns to move forward has reached the peaceful resolve that their loved one is truly in the hands of God and that we have been left here to Live, Laugh, and Love with a passion for each day. Moving forward also means that you may reflect on occasions, but you are not to set back in your emotions that you cannot get up with a smile and thank God for the journey and your future. Destiny becomes your daily diet. Pain is no longer the focus from day to day, week to week, but becomes the stepping stone to fulfill the vision and purpose of God that set in motion. You may experience moments of sadness, but an even greater anticipation of experiencing life at its fullness becomes a motivator.

I started writing this book a few months after my husband passed. Although it was therapeutic, at that stage in my journey, in retrospect I realize that my focus was more on surviving and searching for direction on how to manage my life and my emotions. Writing my story certainly could have served as the vehicle to release pain and encouragement to others.

However, I am so glad that I waited. It has now been over seven years. God revealed that the seventh year was my release from all of the struggles associated with my loss that may have hindered my moving forward. Many things have taken place during the past seven years. I am thankful that I now have a better perspective of the healing process. Therefore, I can give insight to someone who may be in the beginning stages of grief and healing. Or perhaps some years have passed, but your desire to move forward from the pain is still a struggle.

I made the decision to include a vivid description of my journey beginning with the day my husband transitioned from this world to his eternal home. As you read this book, I am sure that you will be able to relate to many of the stages I have described. I compare these phases to the phases of a butterfly. Therefore, you will notice images of butterflies at the beginning of each chapter.

The butterfly is an insect that develops from a larva to an adult through the process of metamorphosis, which is a Greek word meaning transformation or change. The larva looks different, eats different and has different desires. It's whole shape and form evolves through four stages, the egg, caterpillar, pupa, and adult. The larva is small and ugly and very vulnerable. The adult is beautiful and purposeful as it spreads pollen and aids in the reproduction of other flowers and plants. The butterfly is often used symbolically to represent new life, a new beginning, and transformation. Through each stage of development, the butterfly embraces its environment with the hope that it will move forward to the next phase.

Likewise, I compared the phases of the butterfly to the stages of transformation that comes as you work through the stages of grief. Inevitably, your pain will transform your life. You will never be the same. Just as the larva is ugly and unproductive, pain can feel the same way. However, God is shifting you to higher heights. You are being transformed from glory to glory. Inevitably this journey of healing will lead you to unfold another chapter in your life. A better you will emerge. There is purpose in your pain, so keep it moving!

-Angela Roberts Jones

"I can do all things through Christ who strengthens me."
Philippians 4:13

SECTION ONE
THE GRIEF STAGE

It takes strength to make your way through grief,
to grab hold of life and let it pull you forward.
~Patt Davis

I have no more peace.
I have forgotten what happiness is.
I said, "My strength is gone, and
I have no hope in the LORD." LORD, remember my
suffering and my misery, my sorrow and trouble.
Please remember me and think about me.
But I have hope when I think of this:
The LORD's love never ends; his mercies never stop.
They are new every morning; LORD,
your loyalty is great. I say to myself,
"The LORD is mine, so I hope in him."
~Lamentations 3:17-24 (NCV)

1
THE STORY
Till Death Do Us Part

"If we had no winter, the spring would not be so pleasant: if we did not sometimes taste of adversity, prosperity would not be so welcome."
~Anne Bradstreet

To everything there is a season, a time for every purpose under heaven: A time to be born, and a time to die; a time to plant, and a time to pluck what is planted.
~Ecclesiastes 3:1-2 (NKJV)

June 4, 2008 marked the end of a season in my life and the beginning of a new one. It was the day my husband of twenty-four years and ten months suddenly and unexpectedly passed away from a massive heart attack. We married just two months after our college graduation; therefore, most of my adult life was spent as the wife of one husband. That was a season of my life that I will always cherish, but of course, it was a season. As painful as it was to accept, it was a time in my life that would be no more.

The morning of June 4 started off relatively normal. My daughter, Jessica had to wake up very early for a hair appointment. Raliegh and I got up as well, ate breakfast, and had a conversation about sending Jessica to college and finishing up applications, doctor's appointments, and so on. Then suddenly, in a matter of moments, life changed. After breakfast,

Raliegh decided to take a nap because he wasn't feeling well. Before retiring to the couch for his nap, he came into the kitchen and gave me a hug. The hug was sudden and different from usual. We didn't speak, but he held me so close that I began to ask God to show me how to comfort and love this man. I felt his need and his concerns. I felt the heaviness of his heart. But at the time, I did not understand that he was communicating with God about his journey from this earth. He then quietly laid down on the sofa to take a nap.

Minutes later, I heard the ring of the fax machine. I dashed downstairs to receive the fax we had been waiting on and discussing. While downstairs, I heard him scream out. I froze immediately and stopped to listen. I thought maybe he hit his toe or something. Then it registered after a few seconds; this wasn't a familiar scream. It was more of a loud gasp than scream. I ran upstairs, but he was already unconscious. I screamed out his name as I grabbed the phone to call 911. It did not dawn on me at that moment he was in the middle of a heart attack. I think I was in shock, so it just didn't seem real. As I waited for the ambulance that seemingly took forever, and then watching the paramedics attempt to revive him, I feared the worse. He didn't respond to their efforts. His body went limp; his eyes rolled in the back of his head. I felt that he was gone. But I was praying and hoping that the paramedics could revive him. I tried dialing my children, but I couldn't remember numbers right away. Hindsight tells me that I was hysterical and confused.

THE SEPARATION

Right before my eyes, my husband, friend, lover, companion, and father of my children, greatest supporter, and prayer and ministry partner was gone. He was the one who knew all my secrets and what it took to encourage me, to make me laugh, and yes, to make me sad, happy and angry all at once! The relationship between husband and wife is the most intimate relationship on earth. This was just surreal! "Oh my God, what's happening," I wondered!

Whatever happened to, " I, Angela take you, Raliegh to be my lawfully wedded husband, to have and to hold, from this day forward, for better or for worse, for richer, for poorer, in sickness and in health, to love and to cherish, from this day forward, until death do us part." And of course, "I, Raliegh take you, Angela, to be my lawfully wedded wife." Well, the ultimate happened. Death had now parted us. That was not our decision, but it was God's plan and God's will. After all, why else would it happen?

Many marriages end because couples decide or should I say one of the partners in a marriage decides not to honor the marriage vows. However, to an extent, the human will is a significant influence in that painful decision to separate. But the death of a spouse, in most cases, is totally out of the sphere of human control. In the majority of cases, it goes against the will of the surviving spouse. I realize that there are some extremely troubled marriages of which permanent separation could be a relief. (I pray this is not your circumstance!) However, I believe losing your mate through death adds depth to your pain because it is beyond your control. There is no hope of ever in this life, of coming in contact with the person you have pledged your life and love to. There is, in essence, your will versus God's will. The struggle between the two adds to the pain of the loss. Let's be real, it is sometimes difficult to accept God's will.

THE SEASON TO MOURN

The loss of my husband was by far, the most devastating and painful event I had ever experienced. Losing my mate to death felt like my heart was being ripped out. Not only was there a mental and emotional tearing, but a physical severing that is hard to explain, unless you have experienced it. There were days I literally felt physical pain in my body. I instantly related this pain to grief. Nothing seemed to ease those painful moments. Eventually, it would subside, only to return, sometimes unexpectedly. It was impossible at the time to identify the triggers.

But in spite of the pain and confusion I felt, I knew God would somehow bring me through it. I knew I had to be strong for my children. My children… "Lord, please have mercy on them," I thought, I cried, I prayed. Their hearts and emotions were so young and tender. How could I deal with their grief? But then again, I knew that God was in control and that Jehovah Rapha, the God, who heals, would take control. After all, had we not preached so many times at so many other funerals that He was the God of all comfort? Just as the Apostle Paul assured the Corinthian church that he would comfort them with the same comfort he received from the Lord, this now became my reality. I knew God still had work for me to do. I had to put this in His hands. I had to receive His comfort, just as I had ministered so many times to others.

But how?

As I stood in the hospital "quiet room" waiting for an official word from the doctor on what was going on, I walked the floor and prayed. I tried to leave the room to find out what was going on, but I was in such a state of shock that I couldn't figure out where I was. So I went back to the room and prayed while Jessica was in the restroom. I even began to pray in my prayer language as it uncontrollably leaped from my soul. At some point, I started to feel peace and a calming of my spirit. But suddenly, in the middle of my prayer, I felt another presence in the room. There was no one in the room but me so I knew it was the presence of the Holy Spirit. It was such a calming spirit. As I stopped in the middle of the floor, I asked God if He had brought Raliegh back- or if He had taken him. As the last word came from my lips, I felt something like warm oil flow slowly from the top of my head down my body to my feet.

Yes, God was with us. I felt Him in the room. I felt the tangible presence of the Holy Spirit like running oil move from my head to my toe. A few days later, I realized at the very moment I felt the oil move down my body from head to toe; Raliegh was probably transitioning from life on earth to live with the Lord. God was passing the mantle on to me to move forward in the work of the ministry, which was my purpose. At that very moment, I received an anointing to endure this hardship, to comfort those who were mourning with me, and to move forward and continue to preach the gospel. But, of course, that was not my focus at that moment.

A few moments later, the doctor appeared with the devastating news. They had done all they could to revive Raliegh. I absolutely could not believe what he said. I just dropped to my knees. By now, several of our church members were there. They didn't know what to do. My son Jeremy had an hour drive and was on his way. Jessica had made it to the hallway when she heard the news. She just dropped to the floor in agony. And Tony, (Raliegh, Jr.) - was still in Texas waiting by the phone. Several family members were waiting for news. My God! I couldn't believe this was happening. How could I even express what was going on?

THE DAYS THAT FOLLOWED

The days and moments that followed all ran together. There were floods of visitors, phone calls, letters and condolences from all over the community and the country. I am so grateful for all of these expressions. It was comforting to know that we were in the thoughts and prayers of many people. But, we had very little sleep, funeral arrangements and business responsibilities added to the emotional trauma of the loss. I tried to honor Raliegh's wishes concerning his home going celebration. He said to me on many occasions, "If anything was to happen to me, make my funeral service short and sweet. I don't want too many people standing over me. Let the words said over me be few." He felt that an extended program of choirs, speakers and preachers would be too hard on his family. As ministers, we had witnessed this many times.

Three services were planned, the wake at Greenhill, which he had pastored for nineteen years and loved dearly, became a worship service and not a traditional wake. The second service was held at Faith Outreach, a local church in Clarksville who graciously offered their service and support. The sanctuary was larger than that of Greenhill and was packed out with hundreds in attendance. The third service took place at St. Paul Baptist Church in E. St. Louis, Illinois. That was Raliegh's home church where he grew to know the Lord and served under his beloved Pastor Obie Rush. Then on to the cemetery with Police Escort all the way. What a Home Going! I later learned that many family and friends did not have the opportunity to express personal condolences that caused some disappointment. However, it can be extremely challenging to address all of the people who wish to express personal condolences. Dealing with the death of a loved one is already completely overwhelming. In addition to the grief, it is also challenging to acknowledge all who attended services, sent cards, made phone calls, brought over food, said prayers and the list goes on and on. It still seems like a blur to this very day. Did it happen? Of course it did, Raliegh is no longer here.

Several months later, I was in my classroom with my second grade Music students. One of them asked about Mr. Jones. I decided to explain to them what happened. Many of them began to express sorrow and compassion for what I had experienced since the close of the last school year. I explained that I was okay and that God would see my children and me through this season of loss. One student blurted out, "Well we know that death is also a part of life, Ms. Jones, you will be okay." And you know what, that student was right. Death is a part of life, and we will all be okay if we learn how to move on and move forward. Why…because everything in life has a season. There is a time to be born, and a time to die.

SEASONS CHANGE

The beauty of seasons is that they change. It is important to note that all seasons have a set time; the beginning, the middle, and the end. Specific activities characterize each season. God has set the master clock for each season and mother-nature must obey. God's clock was set before the beginning of time as we know it. God's powerful creation still exists in obedience to His perfect will.

The seasons of life bring the experience of good times and bad times, times of sorrow and times of joy, and times of plenty and times of lack. The winter seems cold and unproductive, gloomy and dark. But the winter prepares the earth for the spring and summer seasons. The time that the ground seems barren from the harshness of winter is a time of replenishing the soil. The land goes into a deep freeze, which is a period of rest. If the soil did not rest, it would be overworked and stripped of all of its nutrients. Without winter, there would be no spring.

And so it is with the seasons of life; without grief and sorrow, there would be no real experience of joy and peace. Pain and stress prepare the mind to receive the season of joy and delight, fruitfulness and productivity. The seasons of life are interestingly explained in the third chapter of Ecclesiastes. The author, King Solomon, the Preacher, understood that God was ultimately in charge of the flow and timing of the events in his life. The timing of life cannot be measured in chronological time, but according to God's appointed time for specific things to occur, for all things were created for His purpose. God's timing is not our timing, nor His ways our ways. All things must happen according to the seasons of God's appointed times, which no man has the privilege of knowing. The seasons of life are in the hands of God.

During this season of death and pain in your life, please understand that it will change. Expect change. Look for change. Open your mind to change. Unfortunately, this change in your life at this appointed time has begun with the loss of your loved one. You may cry today, but the season for rejoicing will come. It's all in God's hands. Death is the plan of God to fulfill the purpose of humans as we transition from earth to heaven. There is indeed purpose in the pain of death.

Widowhood is very common. The death of a mate is not something we think about at the wedding. Most newlyweds anticipate growing old together. But inevitably someone has to die first, whether young or old. Very few couples pass away at the same time. It is very common for older couples who have lost a mate to die soon after the other. I can see how the grief of losing a spouse that you have spent over half of your life with can be emotionally and physically overwhelming to the point where you will die from grief. I can also understand how a young newlywed couple can also grieve, not only the loss of a mate but the loss of their future together as man and wife. As I prayed and sought the Lord for wisdom and guidance shortly after the loss of my mate, God gave me the comfort of knowing that the time we lived together as man and wife were all a part of His divine purpose. This season of marriage had a beginning, middle and now an end. A new season had now begun for each of us. Eternal life for Raliegh, but a new season, though painful, had begun for me to continue to fulfill my purpose here on earth. In the words of Job 14:1-6 (CEB);

> All of us are born of women,
> have few days, and are full of turmoil.
> Like a flower, we bloom, then wither,
> flee like a shadow, and don't last.
> Yes, you open your eyes on this one;
> you bring me into trial against you.
> Who can make pure from impure?
> Nobody.
> If our days are fixed, the number of our months with you,
> you set a statute and we can't exceed it.
> Look away from us that we may rest,
> until we are satisfied like a worker at day's end.

MOVING FORWARD

- What is your story? The first step in moving forward is to face the pain.
- Identify a support team that can consist of your pastor, grief counselor (Therapist or Christian Psychologist), family and friends, fellow church members.
- Make time to cry and to mourn. This is the season to grieve. Besides that, tears are cleansing. Releasing your pain is healthy. After crying, shift gears, get up and do something positive.
- Decide from the beginning of this grief stage that you will be healed. There is power in making deliberate choices.
- Survivors are called survivors for a reason. You are a survivor. You are the one still here. Be careful to avoid allowing conversations and activities to become another memorial service. You already experienced one funeral, wake or memorial service. It's time to move past that particular point of grief.
- Make the choice to focus on life and not death.
- Decide that the memories of your loved one will become a source of comfort and not a constant reminder of the pain and loss.
- Start a journal. Write out prayers, reflections, scriptures, dreams, passions, emotions, and everything you are thankful for in life. Always end your entry with a positive praise report of how God is still blessing you.
- Start a scrapbook of cards, pictures, sympathy notes, and so on so that you can reflect when you feel comfortable.
- Give attention to your children and allow them to cry and express their grief and concerns. Identify a support group for them as well.
- Reflect on the memories as you work through this event, but remember; God spared your life so that you can live it. This period of grief will only last for a season. Write it, speak it, pray it, think it. Declare that LIFE MUST GO ON!

THE SUPPORT TEAM

- Listen, Listen, Listen! Allow the one grieving to guide the conversation by providing a safe place for them to vent. Be patient and understanding.
- Your role in the life of the survivor is to comfort them. They are the one in your presence, not their loved one who has passed. Focus on their needs at this particular time.
- At this stage, allow the one grieving to face the pain and reality of the loss. Denial can lead to unhealthy grieving.
- Allow the one mourning to cry. This period of mourning is not necessarily a time for you to give advice or discourage them from crying. Just because one is crying doesn't mean that they are crying with no hope. Crying is a normal and healthy response to pain. Just give them a few Kleenexes and sit patiently until this crying spell is over. It will pass.
- If you had a relationship with the deceased loved one, take personal time to grieve so that you can be a source of comfort. Be careful not to dominate the conversation by expressing your personal loss or grief.
- Make a decision to be a breath of fresh air to the one grieving, to the survivor.

FURTHER REFLECTION

How can you foster a healthy and biblical perspective on death as the gateway to eternal life? Read the following scriptures and record your thoughts: 1 Corinthians 15, 1 Thessalonians 4:13, Revelation 21:1-4, Psalm 116:15

2
WHAT NEXT
Trust God Through The Process

"The fear of death follows from the fear of life. A man
who lives fully is prepared to die at any time."
~Mark Twain

Do not fear, for you will not be ashamed; neither be disgraced,
for you will not be put to shame; For you will forget the shame
of your youth, and will not remember the reproach of your
widowhood anymore. For your Maker is your husband, The
LORD of Hosts is His name; and your Redeemer is the Holy
One of Israel; He is called the God of the whole earth.
~Isaiah 54:4-5(NKJV)

The first forty days immediately after Raliegh's passing were spent in corporate prayer. There were questions as to what would happen to the church such as; who should preach, who would be the next pastor, and so on. Of course, we were grieving and putting the pieces together. People on the outside seemed to be more concerned than we were. The church and my family all realized that we needed to seek God for peace and comfort. We needed to mourn, and we needed to heal.

My primary focus at the time was to make decisions concerning my own personal business. I began to experience first-hand, how difficult it is to close up someone else's life. It is a tedious and challenging process that takes months and in some cases years to complete. These responsibilities also add to the grief phase. When two people become one flesh, in most cases, material assets are listed in both names. Therefore, for me to conduct business, I now had to present the death certificate. In some cases, this was a trigger to the pain of my loss. Psychology suggests that you should avoid making major decisions if possible right after a grief event. I certainly agree with this. Grief is a very powerful emotion that can cloud your ability to think clearly and make good sound decisions.

You may not have the concerns that I faced, but I would advise anyone who loses a loved one to set specific times to pray and free your thoughts. Talking to a trusted friend or family member, therapists, and your pastor can be a tremendous help in explaining your thoughts and giving sound advice. There are other professionals such as financial counselors and lawyers who can help you make sound decisions. I believe in prayer and the power of God. However, God has also endowed people with skills to enable and empower others. I did not seek out a grief counselor, but anytime I needed advice; God led me to the right people.

Whenever anyone asked me about my personal plans or about the plans of the church, we all explained that we were in forty days of mourning and prayer. That helped to avoid uncomfortable conversations and the pressure to make decisions. But it also gave time for God to speak and give clarity to His will and purpose. This prayer time of stillness and listening to God gave us guidance on resources to assist with our decisions.

We began discussions on the length of mourning, and the selection of a pastor at the end of the forty days. It was during this time that I received confirmation from God on His call for me to assume the pastorate. Before his passing, Raliegh mentioned to me on at least two occasions that if something happened to him, I would become the next pastor of Greenhill. He was prophesying and preparing me for this very moment. Well, of course, I dismissed it at the time because I did not think that he would pass away. But low and behold, God was speaking to him. He knew that he only had a little time left to live. There were physical warning signs that Raliegh brought to my attention, such as pain in his left side and the overwhelming feeling fatigue and sluggishness. However, the doctor's report indicated that although the risk factors were present, everything recommended to prevent a significant onset of any illness was working.

God confirmed my call, but I wasn't ready to move forward. I wanted to wait. I wanted to mourn and figure out what to do with my life. I needed to help my children become stabilized emotionally. But the time came that we were forced to make a decision because of the circumstances. The forty days of prayer was not my time, but God's time of waiting for my "yes." It was his time to prepare us all for His plan. There is always a "what next" that we may not calculate into the grief stage. However, God is in charge and walking with you through the tears and the fears of the unknown. He is moving you forward although it may not seem like it at the moment, one day at a time, one step at a time.

You may be dealing with a decision that involves your family and your career. You may not feel ready for the change that God has presented in your life as a result of the loss of your loved one, but God is ultimately in control of this season. You must trust that His plans for your future are good.

I briefly contemplated going back to Georgia near my family. But deep in my heart, I heard the voice of God remind me of particular times of revelation years before this moment. I had to carry the mantle and continue in the vineyard. God called me to the ministry. The anointing had not left me. As a matter of fact, even through tears, I could feel an intense presence of the Holy Spirit in me. I began to pray daily, "I can do all things through Christ who strengthens me." Can you relate? God speaks through the pain. His presence is often stronger during these times to ensure you that He is near.

A few months after Raliegh's passing, I was officially installed as pastor. From the time his passing, and before the Affirmation Service, I continued to render some leadership. I was still serving as co-pastor, but our church family had not made an official decision as to how we would move forward from this. I realized that if circumstances were different, had it been the other way around concerning gender, this would not have been an issue. God used these events to blaze a trail to set forth His purpose not just for me, but for our church and the kingdom. God's plans are comprehensive and expansive. There is always a larger picture. Your circumstances are not just for your experience, but to also play a role to fulfill the destiny of others around you. Your life is just one piece of God's puzzle.

GOD'S FOREKNOWLEDGE

God knows the end from the beginning. The very hairs on your head are numbered. His thoughts of you are precious and are many. There is much more to losing a loved one than the death event. Therefore, God knows the outcome. He knows all of your concerns, and all of the burdens you must bear through this trial.

In my case, I carried the weight of the death of my husband, a mourning church, and the eyes of my community. The question was, "Who would become the next pastor and how would the church handle this?" Some told me of the concern that I needed time to grieve. There were those who were afraid that I could not handle this level of responsibility because of the grief. And secondly, there were those who were concerned and totally against a woman becoming the pastor, even though I had served as Co-Pastor for several years. I thought to myself, "Oh Lord, here we go again." I had become the first female minister licensed and ordained in my church. Now I was becoming the first woman to become pastor, but not in the way that most new pastors were chosen. I became the pastor after losing my husband – in the middle of grief. I believe that this was God's plan all along. God is not a last minute God. He does not react to human events. He is the supreme ruler. His foreknowledge of His Creation guides the events of our lives, and of the world.

When the prophet Jeremiah faced uncertainty about his call because of his youth, God spoke the words: "Before I formed you in the womb, I knew you, And before you were born I consecrated you; I have appointed you a prophet to the nation" (Jeremiah 1:9). This scripture helped acknowledge the fact that I did not become pastor solely because of the death of our pastor, my husband. On the contrary, this was God's plan from the time my mother and father conceived me. In your struggle through the pain of losing a loved one, it is imperative that you acknowledge God's sovereignty and foreknowledge of who you are to become. Understanding that there is purpose in the pain helps to manage the pain. God's intended purpose is like a soothing balm administering Divine pain management.

Some could not accept this change, so they moved to another church. These events are significant because I felt at the time that some of the very ones who cried over the casket and even wept in the hospital room immediately after the passing of their pastor could not find the strength and compassion to stand beside his family in this hour of bereavement. But, God knew this ahead of time. Here we were grieving in a glass bowl with an added weight of making a major decision on the future leadership. However, I can truthfully say at this point that I am grateful for restoration and forgiveness. All of us had to stand before God and some eventually before each other so we could all move forward in love with a clear conscience.

During the time of the forty days, God led me to study the scripture found in Isaiah 54. This scipture brought immediate comfort and guidance as I began to take one day at a time. Moving forward without my mate beside me was overwhelming. I would have to carry the weight of my family and the church by myself, as a single woman. But I had to be obedient. I had to trust God and lean on his almighty power. After all, is this not what we preach…God is able?

In Isaiah 54, the prophet Isaiah uses the metaphor of marriage to describe God's loving care and relationship with the Israelites. In this scripture, God's role as a husband is defined as one who has fulfilled his duties to his wife. He made a covenant agreement with Israel as a pledge of His love, protection and provision for them as long as they obeyed the law. The Israelites experienced widowhood, mainly due to their disobedience and rejection of God's loving role as husband. As a result, they lost their covering, their security and the blessings of peace and prosperity. However, Isaiah 54 is a promise of restoration because God had joined Himself to the Israelites.

Likewise, marriage is the joining of two people who vow to share their lives and everything it entails on a daily basis. Two people become one because their individual destinies become united through marriage. When a man and woman adjust their personal agendas to leave and cleave to each other, an incredible bond is formed that is not easily broken. Many people struggle in marriage because they don't allow this essential element of bonding. But when you take this principle to heart and live it out through your relationship, not only is it rewarding, it makes being torn apart difficult. The awareness of this bond is greater in the loss of a spouse. God created the man to be the provider and protector. The role of the husband is to love his wife and to help her fulfill her purpose. Likewise, the wife is required to do the same. She is to support and respect her husband as she stands beside him as a helpmate. The presence of a godly man brings security and comfort to his wife. That is what I experienced. I didn't realize the magnitude of this until it was taken. However, through Isaiah 54, God reassured me of His promises. I relied on my earthly husband as a covering, but now, I had to rely on God in ways I had never imagined.

GOD'S SECURITY

Raliegh and I were both sophomores in college when we met. We were married two years after we met, and two months after graduation. I was married the majority of my adult life. Losing my mate so suddenly caused a sense of insecurity and loss of protection and provisions. I am an intelligent and independent woman. I know how to take care of myself. But God blessed me with a mate who filled the role of a husband as He intended. When I lost that, I had to deal with these emotions, although they were very subtle. Security concerns are common for all women. I now understand where grief and fear meet. The loss of a loved one magnifies the uncertainty of the future. Fear breeds in the unknown.

I have talked with some of my male friends who are widowers who likewise experienced a sense of insecurity in a different way. Their sense of security came from having their wife as the object of their focus on providing and expressing the love of one who covers. The wife is a nurturer and loves her husband by being a helpmate. It's amazing that God ordained marriage to express what He put in us. Uncertainty comes as the surviving spouse is now required to adapt to a seemingly forced change in the rhythm of life.

Raliegh wasn't perfect, but neither was I. As a matter of fact, there were days that I felt that I couldn't live with him, and other days that I felt that I couldn't live without him. There were times when staying married was challenging and stressful. There were seasons of wedded bliss and seasons of wedded hit or miss! I praise God that we learned how to forgive and endure the trials of marriage. But don't we all experience that in marriage? I just have to smile when I think about it. Thank God for His grace and power. I have to say, that overall, I had a solid and loving marriage.

For a woman, the loss of a good husband is the loss of security in many ways, no matter how independent or self-reliant (as I was and still am) she is. When a man fulfills his role as God intended, (although important), financial security is not necessarily the major concern, but there is security in knowing that whatever you experience in life, you will go through it together. Partnership in marriage is the key to a successful marriage. There is someone to turn to, to cry with, and to laugh with. The future is secure because the two become one in working out the plans for how to live out their God ordained purpose. It is comforting to know that someone – your mate – has your back; and that when adversity comes, you will work through it together.

Although I believe that marriage should be a partnership, traditionally the husband makes sure the house, children, and his wife are provided for in every way. It's a man thing! To have that suddenly taken away is devastating. It is something that is taken for granted until it happens. As I read Isaiah 54, the first thing that arrested my attention was that God referred to himself as the husband and the Israelites as His wife. I have read and studied this passage many times, and even developed sermons. But it had never resonated with me as it did during this season in my life. I realized that my relationship with God had now moved to another level. God was speaking to me directly through this scripture.

The principles of God described in verse five brought immediate comfort to me as I prayed for the wisdom and strength to move forward. Isaiah first says that "your Maker" is your husband. I have described the role of an earthly husband, but imagine that your Creator, the one who knows about you from the inside out, as your husband. Noone knows you as God does, not even your huband or wife. Furthermore, King David expresses in Psalm 139 the awesomeness of God's intimate knowledge. Verses 1-6 reads:

> LORD, you have examined me. You know me. You know when I sit down and when I stand up. Even from far away, you comprehend my plans. You study my traveling and resting. You are thoroughly familiar with all my ways. There isn't a word on my tongue, LORD, that you don't already know completely. You surround me—front and back. You put your hand on me. That kind of knowledge

is too much for me; it's so high above me that I can't fathom it. (CEB)

Just imagine that God, your husband, and maker knows all of your thoughts, your decisions, your fears and doubts, your dreams and desires, your strengths and weaknesses, your concerns and challenges before you can even think or express them.

Furthermore, Isaiah 54:5 describes God the husband as LORD of hosts. He is not just our Maker, but He is the self-existing God, Jehovah, who is the Creator of every living being, both heavenly and earthly. God is the Redeemer or the one who is responsible for reconciling our souls back to Him. Because He is the God of the whole earth, there is absolutely nothing on earth that does not submit to His authority.

GOD THE PROVIDER

Immediately after losing my husband, my protector, and provider here on earth, I had to assume the responsibility of taking care of my children, the house, the car, the bills, all business affairs, and then some. I must admit that although we worked together and discussed things, I managed my share of household affairs. But I had a life partner. I didn't have to carry that load alone. We both had strengths and weaknesses. We brought balance to each other. There were people I didn't have to talk to or even deal with because my husband did it. I didn't make all of the decisions alone because that's what you do in a marriage. The point that I am making is that the loss of this balance subconsciously brought a little fear and apprehension on how to move forward and make some decisions. At the time, I did not acknowledge this emotion as fear, but as time passed, I realized that there was some apprehension lying deep within.

But I have to speak to the real deal – truth to power as they say! I appreciate my personal relationship with God; however I must admit that I missed the presence of the man that God had given me for almost twenty-five years. There is a struggle when you have become accustomed to marriage and all that it entails. You might compare this to the concept of eating three meals every day. If this is a regiment, and you suddenly stop eating, your body will cry out for food. The longer you go without food, the more uncomfortable and challenging it is for the body. Your brain has to adjust to the fact that you are not eating three meals so that your flesh will no longer cry out for the food. Likewise, you will experience similar withdrawal symptoms from the emotional and physical relationship with the loss of a mate. Adjusting to this hole is tough. The loss is severe. The hole is so deep that it seems impossible at the time to fill.

But God, in all of His infinite wisdom and power, can not only fill in the hole and close the gap, but He can ease the emotional and physical hunger that comes from that loss. I will not go so far as to say that I don't need a man, as I have heard some women say. But I do know that God can do exceedingly abundantly above all that we could ever ask or think. I believe that God made man and woman to be dependent on each other on many levels. Marriage was ordained by God from the beginning of His creation of man and woman. He gave us these emotional and physical desires for one another. What better person to help mend the wounds of grief that causes such pain in this area than the God who made us? It takes time, prayer and faith to walk through the process of allowing God to move you forward from the focus of your pain to the focus of your purpose and future.

The healing was easier and more expedient as I began to concentrate more on encouraging and bringing comfort to others. I also began to search deep inside myself to recover gifts and dreams that were lying dormant as a result of focusing on the past on marriage, my husband and children (which is normal for most wives and mothers). I asked the Lord time and time again about the "what next" in my life. I knew that the answer was to fill this gap in a healthy way.

God assured me that through the power of His Holy Spirit, whatever I needed to move forward, He would supply. What more can you ask than to have "your Maker" as your husband! He would help me identify the "what next." By all means, I miss the intimacy of an earthly husband, but oh what a blessing to have God, "my Maker" as my protector and provider. He knows me inside out and will make sure I move to my "what next." Knowing this took away the fear of the unknown.

MOVING FORWARD

- It is comforting to know that not only is your loved one in the hands of God, just as you are but that their death did not catch them by surprise.
- Meditate on God's goodness every day.
- Your loved one moved forward to their eternal home because God prepared them for this transition. In essence, life did not stop for them. Therefore, you are released to move forward, because they too were released to move forward to their eternal home.
- Praise God with great anticipation for the "what next" of your life.

THE SUPPORT TEAM

- Please be mindful that your role in leading the one grieved to a positive and praise of God outlook on life is very influential.
- Avoid comments like 'he's in a better place now" or "you have so much to be thankful for." The one grieving realizes that, but they need you to acknowledge their emotions as valid during this delicate stage.
- There is no set time for grieving. Everyone grieves differently. Avoid giving the one grieving advice on how they should behave during this period.
- Offer practical assistance such as running errands, helping with the kids or cleaning their home. Anything you can do to relieve the load of responsibility can be helpful.

FURTHER REFLECTION

How does God care for you? Read the following scriptures and record your thoughts: Psalm 139, Ephesians 5:22-33, John 14:1-4, 25-28, Isaiah 54

SECTION TWO
THE HEALING PROCESS BEGINS

"Our wounds are often the openings into
the best and most beautiful part of us."
~David Richo

"Hearts are breakable"... "And I think even when
you heal, you're never what you were before."
~Cassandra Clare

Now a certain man was there who had an
infirmity thirty-eight years. When Jesus saw
him lying there, and knew that he already had
been in that condition a long time, he said
to him, "Do you want to be made well?"
The sick man answered Him, "Sir, I have
no man to put me into the pool when the
water is stirred up; but while I am coming,
another steps down before me."
Jesus said to him, "Rise, take up your bed
and walk." And immediately the man was
made well, took up his bed, and walked.
John 5:5-8

3

MAKE AN ADJUSTMENT
Trust God's Master Plan

> God grant me the serenity
> to accept the things I cannot change;
> the courage to change the things I can;
> and the wisdom to know the difference.
> ~Reinhold Niebuhr (Serenity Prayer)

> For the Lord has called you like a wife left alone
> and filled with sorrow, like a wife who married
> when young and is left," says your God.
> ~Isaiah 54:6 (NLV)

What happens when life takes another turn; when your expectations do not come to pass? How do you handle disappointment when the plans you made for your life do not come to pass? How do you manage the pain of shattered dreams and broken expectations? No matter how hard we may try to control life, unplanned events are inevitable. There are circumstances that we cannot change. Can you reverse the death of a loved one? The truth of the matter is that God's plan is THE plan for our lives. He is our Sovereign Creator. Nothing happens in life without first passing through His hands. We live from day to day, with our plans for a beautiful and prosperous future without considering the possibility of shattered pieces and broken dreams.

Several years ago, after the birth of my children, I began to experience back pain. I went to several doctors and tried medications. The approach to treatment by my chiropractor was different than that of traditional doctors. He explained that his approach was a wholeness approach that excluded bandaging the problem by only treating the symptoms with medication. Because the spine and the vertebrae held the entire body together, he further explained that the key to total restoration was to make an adjustment to the spine. Similarly, the key to healing and perseverance in life is to accept the things that we cannot change and to change the things that we can.

I learned that the spine, if not aligned properly, affects other organs in the body. What an education! I immediately reflected on being in my Biology class in high school, which my father just happened to be the teacher! The cure for healing the pain in my back was not to numb the pain but treat the root of the pain by making an adjustment to my posture and bone structure. This fact is important because the bone structure supports the entire body. I learned that as a result of realigning my spine, the healing of other ailments in my body would also take place.

In a similar fashion, I began to recognize that not only did I experience the healing of grief, but as I surrendered to the Chief Physician, I started experience healing of other issues that lie dormant. God began to deal with the root of my pain, which of course was first and foremost, the death of my husband. However, many other issues accompany the loss of a loved one, some of which are mentioned all through this book. As I began to deal with other matters surrounding my pain and the suddenness of my husband's death, I also reflected on his health challenges, and other concerns he mentioned leading up to his death. The stress of dealing with this, along with other issues surfaced after his death. I realized that I had been on automatic pilot for some time.

The pain of this death event opened the opportunity for me to experience healing in other areas. As I faced other issues that surfaced, my life was being realigned. I couldn't go back and talk to my husband about these concerns. I couldn't reverse the hands of time. I had to speak to God about it through prayer. Through the painful emotions of tears and deep sorrow, I experienced an attitude adjustment and illumination into the essence of life and death. Not only was accepting the death necessary for healing, but I had to say yes to life and adjust to the loss.

Life's crises have a way of bringing out and even causing other ailments! Undoubtedly, this is one of the major reasons why conflict arises in families after the death of a loved one. Other issues surface and take over, many of which are irrelevant to the death event. However, I am grateful that my family drew closer through this process. As a matter of fact, other than God, the backbone of my strength came from the strength and prayers of my family, most especially my parents as well as my mother and father-in-law, who are now both deceased. Of course, my church family was here on the frontline praying. There were people in the community praying.

Comparatively, one of the first steps in correcting my back issue was to make an adjustment to the spine by straightening up the vertebrae. Once the adjustment was made, healing could begin. I had to make several visits before I experienced results. Biology teaches us that the body is designed to heal itself, given the conditions of proper diet, rest, and exercise. If these elements are missing, the body struggles to heal itself. Therefore, we must cooperate with our healing by participating in activities conducive to healing.

Let's now compare this process of healing to the emotional trauma of losing a loved one. As God began to align the spine of my heart and soul to His love and purpose, other areas of my life started to fall in line. I realized that a better "me" was emerging. The more I ran to the throne of God, the more I experienced His grace and mercy, revelation and power. Just as I surrendered to the chiropractor's physical manipulation of my spine and vertebrae, I had to surrender to God's divine manipulation of the internal structure of my soul.

The healing process begins as you give attention to the trauma. To make the necessary adjustments, you must face the pain, embrace recovery and face all of the issues unearthed by this trauma. Metaphorically, if the hand is wounded, then pay attention to the hand and not the foot. In other words, stay focused on what is needed to heal at this particular point in your life.

According to Webster's Dictionary, trauma is defined as an experience that produces psychological injury or pain; or a body wound; or shock produced by sudden physical injury. We sometimes overlook the fact that shock to your system or way of life causes injury to the heart and soul, and needs special attention.

For example, the shock of losing a spouse (or any loved one for that matter) can cause fear, anxiety, low self-esteem, depression, confusion, sleeplessness, hopelessness, unforgiveness, bitterness and wrath, frustration, guilt, fear of being alone and the trauma of making decisions on your own. Just as there is physical injury, there is an emotional damage. The military uses the term, Post-Traumatic Stress Syndrome, or PTSD. However, I learned that any individual who has experienced trauma in their life can have PTSD. It takes courage and determination to face issues that can sometimes seemingly bring more pain. However, in the long run, giving attention to these accompanying issues will prove to bring total healing.

ACCEPT WHAT GOD ALLOWS

Immediately after my loss, I realized that to make an adjustment I had to accept the fact that an adjustment had to be made. To heal and move forward, you must take what God has allowed. Moving forward means to deal with the issue head on – first and foremost. Accept the fact that this death, this loss, this pain is real and allowed by God. Death is something you cannot fix. You have to adjust. The memory of having my mate present was good. But accepting the fact that he was gone from this earth, never to return was the key to adjustment. My decisions from then on had to reflect that fact.

Raliegh and I served together in ministry; he was a pastor, and I supported him as co-pastor. We operated as a ministry team. We had counseled the bereaved, conducted funerals, and delivered eulogies among all of the other duties of ministry and marriage. We prayed together and talked about the scriptures. But now, as I faced the death of my loved one, I too had to preach to myself and believe the very words I had spoken to others. Grief became not just a definition, but an experience. I had lost other family members and friends. I had experienced other sorrows and losses. But I had never experienced this type of deep sadness.

During my grief process, I cried, I couldn't sleep, I had headaches, my back and joints ached, and sinus issues flared up periodically. But I knew that he was gone. So I had to accept the fact that I had to go to bed alone, pay the bills alone…, take care of the house, the kids and the car (to say the least)! And then, there was the church! So I had to figure out how to practically manage all of this. All of this was a new norm. Not only were my responsibilities different; I too was different. I had new emotions, new thoughts…, and new feelings. I had never experienced this, but I had to accept it. I took it to God in prayer to help me. There were days that I didn't know what to pray, so I just listened to music and sought to be in His presence. I knew that at these times, the Holy Spirit was making intercession on my behalf. There were moanings and groanings in my soul that I could not utter verbally. I had to learn all over again how to deal with my emotions. Acknowledging emotional changes were critical in those first stages of making the adjustment.

It takes faith and trust in God to accept painful moments in life. Things will not always go your way. Death is as much a divine appointment as birth. What happens in between is due to God's predestined plan for your life, and your choice to live your life to the fullest. You may ask, "Why is this happening to me?" But the question is; why wouldn't it happen to you? Losing a loved one happens to everyone. It's supposed to happen. So, now the question is how will you handle this painful event? Will you search out God's plan with prayerful and positive expectations of excellent possibilities in your future, or will you give in to the pain? Moving forward is a conscious choice. It takes courage to choose life and living even if you are struggling with doubt and fear. The key is to trust that God has the power to transform your life from that of pain to moving forward with purpose and contentment. You may fall, and you may face more disappointments, but you cannot be afraid to accept what God has allowed and make some adjustments.

TIME TO RELEASE

When losing a loved one, not only do you release them to God, but you must also release the life you shared on this earth. After the initial shock of losing your loved one, it's now time to reflect on the dynamics of the relationship such as: What did you love most about your spouse? What did you dislike the most? What about him or her triggered your hot button? What about your spouse made you feel complete? What will you miss the most? Are there any unresolved issues between you and your deceased loved one? All of these concerns add layers to the grief and the healing process.

Therefore, to experience total healing, you must release more than just the fact that they have passed. You must let go of a daily routine and lifestyle established as a result of your relationship. You must courageously accept the reality that life will never be the same. The moment your loved one transitioned into a new life from earth to heaven is the very moment you transition into a new life right here on earth. The memories are precious. But they are just memories. There will not be another opportunity to share life's events and create memories with your lost loved one.

Losing your established life and the loved one is painful to accept at first but to make an adjustment; you must receive this very real truth. Some plans did not come to pass, especially when the death is sudden and you are still in the prime of life. You may know it with your mind, but it takes time for the heart to catch up. If you by chance have had a painful experience, are you living in the memory or the reality of it? The reality is that it is over, although the situation may continue to exist in your mind. The more entangled your life was with your deceased loved one, the more intense the pain, that's why losing a spouse is so painful. Marriage unites your entire life to another person.

Accepting the reality that this painful event was just an event, a moment of time in your life propels the healing process. Viewing this experience as an event in your life is not belittling the significance of the trauma, but it is still just an event. You may have experienced, not just the death of a spouse, but the loss of a parent or child, divorce, betrayal of a friend or significant other; church hurts, job loss, rape, molestation, or illness. Even growing older presents an important life change, often gradually, but sometimes instant.

However, the reality of most significant life events is that it is not something that will happen every day of your life. No condition in life is ever permanent. It may be painful, but it is still a moment in time, a defining moment in the big scheme of life. Traumatic events are just one piece to a puzzle with many pieces. Emotional damage takes place during a traumatic event, but you will heal after you accept what happened. It will become "a former" thing, life will be different. You can choose to hold on and remain in a state of perpetual grief, or you can embrace new possibilities for your life. Reflect on the lessons learned through this experience and allow them to propel you to move to greater heights.

Consider this profound principle found in Numbers 33:53 and 55: (NKJV)

> ...You shall dispossess the inhabitants of the land and dwell in it, for I have given you the land to possess. But if you do not drive out the inhabitants of the land from before you, then it shall be that those whom you let remain shall be irritants in your eyes and thorns in your sides, and they shall harass you in the land where you dwell.

This particular scripture refers to the children of Israel and their journey to the Promised Land. God admonished them to drive out their enemies so that they could possess His promise and fulfill their God-given destiny. Now let's compare this to grief and mourning. The grief state of mind, if left untouched will be an irritant as your strive to move forward. These emotions will serve as harassment, a constant reminder of the pain and loss that you experienced. If you don't make an adjustment, you will be shackled to the bondage of pain, or perhaps the symptoms of the painful experience. An adjustment needs to be made to prevent this bondage.

I have met people who fall into a pit of despair and depression every year for ten – twenty –and even twenty-five years at the anniversary of the death of a loved one. For example, several years ago, I ran into an acquaintance one day while shopping on a beautiful sunny afternoon. When I asked how she was doing, she told me that she wasn't having a very good day. As a matter of fact, she added, she was not having a very good month. When I asked why, she explained to me that her daughter had been killed in a car accident during that particular month fifteen years ago. She explained that each year, she found herself struggling through that particular month. I said some encouraging words to her, however, to be honest, at that moment, I said a prayer, "Lord don't let that ever be me. I can't see myself grieving for fifteen years!" This encounter was long before I experienced the death of my husband. But it came to my mind after his passing. I cannot fathom grieving in that manner for that long.

Because of their lifelong connection, elderly couples may grieve differently due to their stage in life. But I also believe that it is not God's desire for His children to live in a state of perpetual grief. Memories can be painful and bring momentary sorrow. I have often discussed this with my parents who still feel a twinge of sadness after losing my brother in the early ninety's. We all feel that sense of loss at particular family times because of the connection. However, it comes and goes. The body, soul and spirit are designed to heal itself through the divine guidance and intervention of an almighty and all-knowing God. I don't believe that a day – week or month in a year is declared off-limits indefinitely so that the spirit of grief can come and take you backward in time. It is God's will that His children progress, grow, live, rejoice and glory in the blessings He has bestowed upon us!

REALIGNING TO GOD'S PLAN

In my visits to the chiropractor, my spine was physically adjusted by the doctor. There were times that I could barely walk after an adjustment because it took a little time for my body to conform. Likewise, to align your emotions, you must begin to see yourself beyond this event. You may feel paralyzed emotionally at first, but the mind will catch up, and you will live beyond this event. Make a decision to heal, and do what it takes to get there. What do you want out of life? Where would you like to be in your life six months, one-two or five years from now? What will it take to get there? Do some research and begin moving forward.

An important part of that alignment process is to come into agreement with God on His plan and His purpose for life. Yes, that also means accepting death from a biblical perspective. No one lives forever. Your time on earth is limited. You must make a conscious decision to shift your mind from the pain and uncertainty of your grief event and seek out God's plan for your life. It may take some effort, but it is not that difficult.

One of the major revelations I received in my seeking God for wisdom on how to move forward was the fact that death is personal. I remember praying and asking God about what I could have done differently on the day that my husband passed. Could I have spoken to the 911 operator differently so that they would have moved faster? What could I have done differently? I distinctly remember hearing the Holy Spirit speak audibly to my soul, "Death and life are in the hands of God." In an instant, I was released from the guilt of "what if." We are our Heavenly Father's children. The spiritual reality is that life is between God the Father, and His child. God is our Creator. He is the giver and sustainer of life. Just as every aspect of life is a significant element in our relationship with God, so is every aspect of death. I believe David expresses this perfectly again in Psalm 139, especially verses 13-15:

> You covered me in my mother's womb. I will praise You, for I am fearfully and wonderfully made; Marvelous are Your works, and my soul knows very well. Your eyes saw my substance, yet being yet unformed. And in Your book they all were written, The days fashioned for me, when as yet there were none of them.

Through his trials, David penned this personal revelation that God had already predestined his life. David experienced much affliction, so he questioned God's presence and purpose in all of the pain and suffering. I pray that you receive this revelation that God predetermined who you would be by creating you from the inside out, before your days on earth began. Your personality, gifts, skills, and talents were predetermined. Although life is full of choices, you were chosen by God before you were in your mother's womb. And so was your spouse, or loved one. Neither his /her life, nor his /her death was in your hands, but in the hands of God.

God made an excellent creation when He formed you and me. He saw your life from the beginning to the end.

He carefully designed and planned out your days so that every detail would aid in the fulfilling of your purpose here on earth.

Your days are numbered.

Your days are fashioned. They are predetermined by the potter who has skillfully crafted you and me on the potter's wheel. Only God can foresee what happens between birth and death. It is our choice to submit to God's master plan, especially when it doesn't match our own.

What does this have to do with the loss of your spouse? Well, just as your life is in the hands of the potter, so was the life of your spouse (or loved one). He/she belonged to God first. God numbered their days. There may not have been anything YOU could have done differently to prolong their days. At the end of the day, we all have to stand before our Maker and face HIS master plan for life, and death. The healthy and sure way to make an adjustment and move forward in the healing process is to accept this very thing. Death and life both lie in the hands of the Almighty! This belief is very liberating and opens the door to a healthy, hopeful, and happy expectation of the days that lie ahead.

MOVING FORWARD

- As you move through the healing of grief, it is best to avoid making firm or permanent changes such as selling your home, changing jobs, moving to another city, or making major purchases. Make adjustments as needed, one day at a time as God's will for your life is confirmed, and your mind becomes clear.
- Make sure you open all of the blinds and clean the house. It is also important to eat a good hearty meal, at least once a day if not three times daily. Drink a lot of water and fluids.
- Put the pictures of your loved one in a drawer, turn them down or put them in a room that you are very seldom in, if only for a day so that you can focus on something else. You can put them back until you make a permanent decision on what to do with them.
- Grief is already consuming, so make up your mind that you will take control of your life and schedule other activities in your day on purpose. Try to avoid allowing your grief to drive or dictate your day.

THE SUPPORT TEAM

- Help the one mourning to shift from tears of sorrow to tears of laughter. Laughter is good medicine for the soul.
- The one mourning should now begin to examine the reality of the death of their loved one and how it has affected their life in practical ways, such as talking every day.
- Offer your support by asking what can you do to help them make the necessary adjustments to a new way of life.

> Understand that you don't always have to know what to say. Express that and exercise the ministry of presence. You can share in the moment by being a comforting presence and support.
> The person you are comforting needs normal conversations about normal life so that they can get back to the normalcy of life.

FURTHER REFLECTION

Discuss or write specific steps needed to adjust life without the deceased loved one. Formulate a daily plan that will reflect the needed changes. Read the following scriptures and record your thoughts: Isaiah 40: 28-31; Isaiah 43:1-2; Proverbs 3:5-6,

4

KEEP IT MOVING
In Spite of the Pain

"I thank God for my handicaps, for through them
I have found myself, my work and my God."
~Helen Keller

Also the word of the LORD came to me, saying, "Son of man, behold, I take away from you the desire of our eyes with one stroke; yet you shall neither mourn nor weep, nor shall your tears run down. Sigh in silence, make no mourning for the dead; bind your turban on our head, and put your sandals on your feet; do not cover your lips, and do not eat man's bread of sorrow. So I spoke to the people in the morning, and at evening my wife died; and the next morning I did as I was commanded.
~*Ezekiel 24:15-18 (NKJV)*

When does the healing begin, and when does the pain stop, or does it end? After seven years, I can testify to the fact that although there are moments of sad reflections triggered by past memories and situations such as viewing sad movies, the intense lingering pain stops. I believe that the grace of God has not only brought healing but has also opened my eyes to a new perspective on life and death. Knowing that I have experienced this trauma keeps me grounded and humbled by the progress from the beginning of this process of healing to now. I appreciate the process of healing and the totality of wholeness infused into every area of my life.

The reality is that although it may not feel like it, the healing process begins immediately after the trauma. The presence of pain does not mean that healing is not taking place, but rather, it brings attention to our humanness and need for our Creator and Father God to administer His healing balm.

Through this process, I discovered that we as humans are more in tune with God's presence when we are hurting. We are groping and seeking God to rescue our desperate need for His loving and healing hands. It is through this process that God's purpose for our lives begins to speak profoundly. Tears are an expression of an open heart. An open heart is what God needs to project His will, wisdom and power to cause us to move forward on purpose.

I can't say that I was physically handicapped like Helen Keller, who was both deaf and blind, but grief can temporarily, and even permanently in some way, handicap our emotions. The overwhelming experience of sorrow potentially causes a numbing effect on the emotions. This emotional impairment can stifle one's ability to adequately perceive the world around them, and can, in turn, disable your ability to move forward. To be handicapped simply means that some part of the body, soul or spirit lacks the capacity to function fully. We would all be permanently disabled to the point of not fully operational if it were not for the grace and mercy of God who gives us supernatural strength.

A fitting illustration of God's grace is found in 2 Corinthians 12:7-10. The Apostle Paul speaks of a thorn in his flesh that he petitioned God to remove. He describes it as a messenger of Satan sent to humble him. After pleading before the Lord in prayer three times, he realized that he would have to function and fulfill his divine call although the thorn would not be removed. Jesus' response to his petition was, "My grace is sufficient. My strength is made perfect in weakness." In spite of this very real challenge in Paul's life, he fulfilled his call as an apostle.

In reading this passage, we should note that Paul was a real person who was emotionally distraught over his condition. However, he did not stop. Paul kept moving and fulfilled his destiny. He trusted God one day, one step at a time. He was not alone; God was with Him.

Likewise, this is relevant to not only the loss of a loved one but other life challenges that cause pain and grief. In my case, the loss of my husband was a challenge. He was gone, never to return. This thorn of pain and loss was real. However, God supplied the strength to keep moving and fulfill His call on my life to encourage and empower others. God's grace was and still is sufficient. He is the same yesterday, today and forever. His love, grace, and mercy are everlasting. His faithfulness endures forever. He created you, and He will see you through to the very end of your journey, just as He has seen me through.

When it comes to the event of loss, keep in mind that the memory of the event will never go away. You will never forget your loved one. But God's grace is sufficient to empower you to keep it moving. Furthermore, God's grace is so powerful, that you can and will by faith become healed completely. The God of all comfort is faithful. Thank God for His grace.

PREVAILING PURPOSE

Another excellent biblical illustration of someone who kept it moving can be found in Ezekiel 24:15-27. The prophet Ezekiel was told by God that "the desires of his eyes would be taken away with one stroke." Of course, God was referring to Ezekiel's wife. Ezekiel would prophesy in the morning, his wife would die in the evening, and he was to get up the next morning and continue to prophesy as he was assigned and anointed by God to do. God instructed Ezekiel not to display publicly the traditional signs of mourning, which included intense sorrow through crying, removing his turban and covering his head and face with ashes, covering the face, removing the sandals and walking barefoot. This tradition was not only practiced to show public mourning as an expression of grief, but also as a memorial for the deceased.

God expressly instructed Ezekiel to continue his ministry assignment and speak oracles to the people. He was only to sigh in silence. There was a predominant purpose for these explicit instructions. The people were living in Babylonian exile due to God's judgment for their disobedience. The prophet Ezekiel was among those chosen to ensure that the people remained connected to God and obeyed his message. They would lose everything precious to them, the desire of their eyes, the pleasure of their souls, their sons and daughters would fall to the sword. However, they were not to mourn (v. 20-23). God says to the people in v. 24, "Thus Ezekiel is a sign to you; according to all that he has done you shall do; and when this comes, you shall know that I am the Lord GOD."

"Was Ezekiel as vulnerable as any other human being to grief and pain?" one might ask! We sometimes fail to realize that the biblical characters were human and that their stories are real. We can safely conclude that Ezekiel experienced every bit of the sorrow and pain that you and I experience when we lose a loved one, most notably, the "desire of your eyes" as God refers to Ezekiel's wife. These very words spoken by God indicate that He recognized the delight and affection that Ezekiel felt about his relationship with his wife. From what we can assume about a pleasurable marriage, it is safe to imagine that she apparently brought joy and comfort to Ezekiel's life. The presence of his wife undoubtedly brought a measure of security and support to his ministry. I am sure that she was his personal prayer partner and confidant.

However, although Ezekiel experienced sorrow, God instructed him to exhibit self-denial and allow purpose to prevail over grief. In the midst of great affliction, God empowered Ezekiel to submit to His authority and His will. Ezekiel's life became an illustration of God's message, and of God's grace. I can't say that the call on my life is the same as that of Ezekiel's, but I can somewhat relate to Ezekiel's loss and assignment. I lost my husband, but I had to continue in my assignment.

Although my reflection on Ezekiel's life has been chiefly, ministry focused, please understand that one's purpose in life far exceeds vocation, careers and even the call of ministry duties, but also includes family and relationships. In my case, the death of my mate came one week after my daughter's high school graduation. We were in the process of preparing for her first year of college. My son was still in college and in the process of working toward graduation. They both continued as scheduled. I was still teaching full time. I went back to work as planned.

Also, on the night before Raliegh's death, we had a community meeting for our annual Back to School Bash. We expected to pack about 5000 book bags with school supplies and service about 2000 needy families. We had a life. Things were going on. Although many things came to a screeching halt after my husband's passing, we couldn't just stop in the middle of life. There was still work to do. We continued to plan for the Bash. We could not overlook the responsibilities, so of course, the work of the ministry continued. Yes, I did delegate, and our church rose mightily to the occasion, but I still found that I could not just stop altogether. In fact, the members who stood with my family and me continued to carry on the work of the ministry. Praise God!

If you are reading this and experiencing the trauma of grief, you may think that it will never end, or that it will never get better, but it will. Don't wait until you feel better to get up and continue with life, keep it moving!

Many people have said to me that my perseverance and endurance inspire them. I was still teaching full time and took on the added responsibility of pastoring full time in the midst of grief. My testimony is; "there is a God." I began to gain strength with every message that I prepared and preached. I was encouraged by every sick visit, and every opportunity I had to motivate and inspire someone else. I was preoccupied with strategic planning and vision for my life and the church. The discipline of fasting, prayer and studying the Word of God strengthened my faith and brought deep cleansing to my soul. God gave me the awesome opportunity also to minister healing to this mourning congregation, who so loved their pastor.

It was not easy. It was sometimes stressful and even brought doubt and fears of inadequacy to all of us. Grief can be incredibly overwhelming. There were times that I asked God, how can I wipe someone else's tears when I have been crying off and on all night? But through the Spirit of God prompting and enabling me to get up from my bed of grief when it hurt the most, the process of healing and strengthening began. Many people have said to me, "if you can do it, I can too." You never know whose watching. Your testimony serves as a trophy of God's grace, and a live example of His miraculous power in action. My personal testimony is that purpose prevails over pain if you surrender to it.

MY EZEKIEL MOMENT

Four months after the funeral, an official service was held to affirm my position as pastor. However, at the end of the forty days after the funeral, I began preaching again. There were several occasions that I found myself in the study before Sunday morning service fighting back tears because something triggered memories. I would say a prayer and go forth. One particular Sunday, I was so heavy that I could not mask it. Without any questions or conversation, a couple of ladies came into the study, grabbed my hands and began to pray. I made it through that Sunday. On another occasion, as I stood up to preach in the pulpit the choir sang fervently in worship before the message, I dropped to my knees in worship and asked God for strength. I began to pray and worship on my knees in tears before regaining my composure to preach. That was a moment of release for the church and me. It was then apparent that they needed to cry with me. We needed to mourn together. This process was cleansing and healing for us. It brought us together in unity because we were all striving to move forward.

In addition to my duties of preaching, I made a rotation schedule for our ministers and elders to step in as needed. I made hospital visits, home visits, nursing home visits, counseled where needed, met with trustees and deacons and other leaders as needed. I was still very actively engaged in the decision-making of our church in every area. Though we were mourning, the business of the ministry did not stop.

About nine months later, one of our members, a twenty-year-old young lady was killed in a car accident. This event was our first experience with death after the loss of our pastor. Furthermore, this was my first experience as the senior pastor to minister to a grieving family and plan a funeral. It was very painful, especially because we not fully healed. This young lady grew up in our church and was very close to my children, one of my daughter's best friends. She had spent a lot of time in my home. She was also the daughter of one of our most faithful ministry couples. It was tragic. It was painful. We were mourning again.

If this were not enough, we began to experience unexpected deaths in our congregation every six to nine months for about three years straight. These successive and sudden deaths were more than I had ever experienced even as the pastor's wife and co-pastor. The point is that even during this time of grief, healing came as I continued with the pastoral duties. Executing the duties of ministering to families was my purpose. I began to experience a great measure of strength and encouragement because my focus was no longer on my pain alone.

Contrary to popular belief, you must give attention to the wound, but you don't have to stop life to do that. The healing process takes place as you continue to move forward with the inspiration of your passions, gifts, skills, and talents. I was called to do this. The process of grief did not negate the call of God on my life; it only enhanced the call and caused me to trust in the power of God, and not myself. Just as Ezekiel was told to get up and prophesy the next morning after the loss of his wife, God instructed me to keep walking in my purpose and calling to fulfill my assignment. This was my Ezekiel moment. God revealed to me that He would enlarge my territory and bless me beyond what I could imagine. So I obeyed and continued to keep it moving. As a result, healing did come. When I am weak, He is indeed strong. That's a fact!

DEFEATING LONELINESS

Loneliness is another obstacle many people face after the loss of a loved one. This particular feeling of isolation can be looked upon as situational loneliness because it comes as a result of your situation. The benefits of marriage include that of companionship and friendship. A companion is someone who keeps you company or accompanies you for various activities and life events. It stands to reason that a person who loses their spouse will automatically experience loneliness and isolation. Some of the triggers for the feeling of isolation include eating alone, traveling, attending social functions, family gatherings, late night conversations, making decisions and everything else you might do with a very close companion.

I recall feeling such a deep hole in my life because my husband was also my friend, which is true of most marriages. My mate was someone who shared my purpose in life. He was interested in my day and listened patiently to my ups and downs. He helped me to become what God had purposed me to be. He was also my prayer partner and spiritual confidant, and the father of my children. At the time, I felt like I lost my biggest supporter. This person knew me better than anyone else in the world, the good, bad and the ugly. He knew my secrets and most things that I had experienced in my adult life up until that point. Likewise, I knew him, his secrets, his desires, his strengths and weaknesses, his ups and downs.

The loss of a spouse is enormous, beyond expression. The presence of a spouse fulfills the human needs of love and togetherness. Every human being has the need to be loved and appreciated. But we also have the need to express love and appreciation for another. The loss of a mate takes away this special opportunity to love and be loved.

Being alone and loneliness are two different things. You can be alone, but not feel lonely. Likewise, you can feel lonely, but not be alone. The presence or loss of a spouse can cause either or both. Because the loneliness that I am speaking of is situational, you may always miss your spouse, but healing will surely come as you make adjustments to your lifestyle.

I believe that we as ministers and Christians, family and friends, sometimes miss the boat when we speak to encourage a person experiencing loneliness such as "you are never alone because Jesus is with you." Of course, this is true. As a believer in Christ, I receive this. But let's be realistic and practical. We are human beings. God created us to be relational and interdependent. It is human and very normal to experience loneliness. We are born into families and operate in the world as communities. God ordains marriage as the foundation for the institution of the family. Families share the same home, the same dinner table, the same space. God created human beings to function this way. Praying and trusting in God surely helps. But the person who loses their mate has to learn to foster healthy relationships with people that will help them adjust to this new life.

I have come to the conclusions that one of the major elements to defeating loneliness is to avoid trying to replace your spouse. Your spouse was a unique individual. You had a special relationship. That relationship will cease because sadly, they have passed away. It is now time to allow God to open the door of opportunity to make new relationships and experience companionship, love and intimacy with others on a new level. Everything must change! Embrace this change as positive and thank God for new relationships.

In my case, I experienced the loss of my husband and the "empty nest" season all at the same time. Initially, I didn't know what to do with myself. I remember praying at home one day and looking up from where I was postured on my knees and thinking, "God, I know that you are up there watching me walk through this house." At that moment, I found that to be a little humorous. From that moment on, I would sometimes laugh out loud as I moved through the house cleaning, reading, watching television, working out or whatever. It's funny because I would find myself in situations that no one would believe. For example, the time a frog got in my house and

I was afraid to touch it. I tried to spray it down with whatever I could find. I thought it would die, but when I went back the next day, it had moved. (There's more to this story, but I won't tell it right now!).

But moving on (LOL!!), another element to combating loneliness is to have the courage to leave the house and go around people, or focus on particular task or hobbies. I love to read, I love listening to music, playing the piano, and I enjoy encouraging others. I enjoy working in the community. But what I found most rewarding at the time was taking the time to visit those who were sick or down and out. My situation caused me to be very sensitive to the broken-hearted, so I found comfort in bringing comfort to others. I received joy and peace by imparting this to others. I also made a decision to initiate calls and connections with others instead of waiting on a call. I realized that this was no time to have a pity party. The purpose in my life gave me the needed motivation to continue moving. I didn't have time to sit in the house and wait on someone to give what God had already given me; that is, wisdom, guidance and the strength to combat this.

Another thing that helped me to avoid succumbing to a state of loneliness was the fact that I was busy being productive and purposeful in moving forward with my personal development. I made a decision to go back to school to study theology. That was a desire that I had for many years but was unable to devote any time to it. Between teaching, pastoring and studying, I had no time to dwell on the fact that I was without a mate. Honestly, this was a good time to accomplish some goals that I had set years back. God has a reason for every season. I embraced this time as "my time" to give God "His time" to take me to another level in life. I still experienced many lonely moments, but I was not alone.

Another accomplishment that helped me to move forward was the project of redecorating my home. It was fun redecorating because my house began to reflect my personality and my preferences. I remember shopping and looking at a couch many years ago that I thought would look perfect in the living room. Needless to say, my husband thought the couch was ugly, so we didn't purchase it. Compromise is the name of the game in marriage!!!

I was now in a different season of my life. It didn't matter what anyone else thought. I didn't have to compromise. I decided that I needed to make things comfortable for me. It was fun and very rewarding to see my vision for my surroundings come to pass. In the process of redecorating, many of the grief triggers vanished. My advice to you is to take note of the things around you that magnify your loss and modify your surroundings. Sometimes, all it takes is another coat of paint or a different color bedspread. Do what you can afford, make a plan, and make that change. I guarantee that you will be so glad you did!

EMBRACE THE PAIN OF RECOVERY

After years of dealing with back pain, I decided a few months ago to have surgery. My doctor explained that the procedure would alleviate pain in addition to bringing a measure of correction so that restoration to other damaged areas could take place. The long healing process would begin long before I would feel completely normal. Although the majority of the pain would disapear in four to six months, the total healing process would take up to a year. However, I noticed that the treatment for healing began immediately following the surgery.

The surgery was very painful and left my body fragile. I also experienced some complications which caused me to wake up from the anesthesia without any pain medication (imagine that). However, the nurses showed up a few hours after the surgery to get me out of bed. Traces of the anesthesia were still in my system, the pain medicine that I eventually received caused a little confusion and sluggishness, but they still got me up out of the bed to walk. The nurses did not allow me to lay in bed for days and weeks. To heal properly, my body had to continue to move and work although it had suffered from the trauma of surgery. The reason for moving so soon after surgery was to avoid stiffness that would cause more pain, and other ailments to set in such as respiratory and digestive issues, and eventually arthritis or other joint issues.

Recovery from any trauma can be very challenging. It was difficult for me to get out of the bed after back surgery. It was painful to go through physical therapy and get back to the routine of life. The recovery process was sometimes uncomfortable and challenging. But I wanted to heal, so I had to endure the discomfort and embrace the recovery plan. However, I knew that the pain of recovery would ensure that I would one day be pain-free. You can apply this same principle to the process of healing for emotional and mental trauma.

Losing a spouse does not end your life. As a matter of fact, your suffering is a perfect opportunity for God to display His glory in your life. God has a recovery plan. It may be painful, but rest assured, you will recover. As challenging as it may be to get up and move forward, you must cooperate with the healing God has already ordained for this season of sorrow.

One of the scriptures that I quoted over and over as I embraced God's recovery plan was, "I can do all things through Christ who strengthens me." (Philippians 4:13). As I quoted this scripture day in and day out, I was consistently reminded that God Himself was giving me the strength to get up each and every day no matter how I felt. I had a purpose. People needed me. I needed them. My purpose, God's purpose was calling! There were things to accomplish and goals to meet. It was on!!! If you are reading this and haven't gotten up, let me encourage you right now to get up. Do you want to be healed? Pick up your bed and walk! Don't wait until you feel like it. The more you move, the better you will feel! A body in motion stays in motion!

MOVING FORWARD

- Be proactive and make out a calendar of events for the week. Just as physical activity can prevent and eliminate pain, actively pursuing your passion, and things that you enjoy will eventually prevent and reduce emotional pain.
- Create new memories, new habits, make new friends, explore a new career, get a new hair-do, lose weight and buy some new clothes, go back to school – read a book or better yet – write one, pick up a new hobby.
- Make new friends and don't be afraid to let go of the old ones that may hinder your progress.
- Do something to reinvent your life. Have confidence in yourself and your abilities, and better yet, have faith in what God has put in you. Take inventory of your strengths, gifts, and talents, as well as your weaknesses.
- Get involved in church. Volunteer in the community. Join a committee on your job. Encourage others, pray for others, visit those who are sick and shut it. You don't want to get busy just to be busy, write out goals with intentional steps, and keep it moving!

THE SUPPORT TEAM

- Share words of encouragement to pursue their dreams.
- We often make the mistake of expecting too much emotionally from the one who is grieving. Just because they don't reach out to you the way you think they should doesn't mean that they don't need you. Keep reaching, keep checking on them, and keep on praying for them. Believe me, they will never forget it, and eventually, you will get a response, most especially if you already have an established relationship.
- You should be concerned if that person stays at home and discontinues interacting with friends, family and the world around them. Lovingly encourage them to continue in life's journey by showing patience and consideration for their state of mind.
- Invite them to dinner or a social event. They may say no today, but they will probably feel different the next time you extend an invitation.
- Keep in mind that the purpose of social outings and gatherings for the one grieving is to take a break from the reminder of grief. There were times I just wanted to enjoy the event without being in the position of talking about my situation. As I began to heal, God revealed to me that the reason I subconsciously avoided certain public events was because I felt very uncomfortable with the spotlight being shined so brightly on my grief and loss.
- You must be mindful that your grief moment is your grief moment. Your time of reflection may not be the appropriate time of reflection for the one you are seeking to encourage. Be prayerful and sensitive to the needs and feelings of the one grieving. They need times of normalcy. God has placed you in the life of the one grieving to encourage and gently remind them to remain engaged in life.

FURTHER REFLECTION

Keep it moving by helping others. Read the following scriptures and record your thoughts: Romans 15:1, Job 17:9, Exodus 17:12, Matthew 25:25-46.

5
GLANCE BACK- GAZE FORWARD
Your Present Pain Will Not Paralyze Your Future

Holding on to pain will empower the pain to hold you back.
~Angela Roberts Jones

No, dear brothers and sisters, I have not achieved it,
but I focus on this one thing:
Forgetting the past and looking forward to what lies ahead.
~Philippians 3:13 (NLT)

To move forward, you must let go of the pain. You may have asked the question, "How do I look forward when my days are filled with overwhelming pain?" Or "how do I look forward when my days are filled with the activities and responsibilities of taking care of my current needs?" This reality is what anyone dealing with grief or emotional pain must face. It is a matter of mental determination and a deliberate decision of where to place your mental energy. It takes courage to make the decision to finally let go of whatever is hurting your heart and soul.

The difficulty in letting go for some people lies in the confusion of whether letting go somehow dishonors the life of your deceased loved one. However, do you think that your deceased loved one is now wondering if you are sitting day after day thinking and brooding over their absence? Why of course not. This very real fact should set you free to remember the past, but live in the present. You must stop and address the pertinent issue of what is real at this moment in time. Who died, you or your loved one?

I discussed this very thing with my daughter one day. She had been in the bed for several days a month or two after the funeral. I was aware of the fact that this behavior is normal during the grief process. However, I was concerned that the sorrow and pain would turn into a state of deep depression. I opened her bedroom door and urged her to get out of bed. She said something to the effect that she couldn't. I then began to share with her that I know this hurts, but I urged her to see herself beyond this event. She was about to begin her freshman year in college. I knew that it would be rough. But somehow, I knew that to survive, she had to get up and look forward. I shared these same thoughts with my son who was already in college at the time. They had their whole lives ahead of them. It would be tough to move forward without their father. But what would they do with the rest of their lives if they didn't? Their father had already lived his life. He made peace with God and fulfilled his purpose here on earth. Those of us left here on earth would have to do the same.

When losing a loved one, understand that you cannot grieve forever. You have to live. Needless to say, eventually, my son Jeremy did graduate. My daughter Jessica did go to school. She ended up starting a business that is now very successful. She has also published her first book. Raliegh, Jr., who has a successful career in the field of technology and ministry, eventually decided to launch back out in ministry to follow his passion and start a church in Texas with the blessing of his pastor. I know that they had lost their father, but they still had a life ahead of them. Taking that first step to dream and envision yourself in the future begins the journey to move forward.

The Apostle Paul presents the concept of moving forward in the third chapter of Philippians. Paul lists his accomplishments and credentials at the beginning of the chapter. According to verses five and six, these achievements gained respect for Paul among his peers. On the contrary, he also gained the ruthless reputation for being a persecutor and murderer of Christians. However, he reiterates that he had no confidence in the flesh, that is, those accomplishments that brought him social status. His goal was to become more like the Lord and to attain the salvation of Jesus Christ.

Therefore, he stressed that his worldly accomplishments and past mistakes were irrelevant at that point to moving forward. He could glance back, but he had to gaze forward to God's ultimate purpose. As Paul yielded his life to the purpose of preaching the gospel that God had ordained for him, he realized that whether right or wrong, his past was not the end goal of his life. In other words, he had to appreciate the past for what it was at the time – his past. His accomplishments were notable for that time, but he was pressing toward the desired goal that had already been laid out by him because of the sacrifice of Jesus Christ.

Through his struggles, God was able to capture his attention to reveal his intended purpose. As a result of Paul's revelation of Jesus Christ and his calling, he chose to forget those things that were past and gone, and press forward. I like the fact that he uses the term press. This word depicts the fact that it just didn't happen; Paul had to make a decision and work to move toward his desired goal. He had to press or move with force and intentionality through anything and everything, the beatings and betrayals, the imprisonment and physical fatigue to attain the goal of ultimate salvation and obedience to His purpose.

PUTTING THE PAST IN PERSPECTIVE

Now to forget those things that were behind (as mentioned in this scripture) did not mean that Paul could erase events and experiences from his memory. It merely meant that he had to put it in its proper perspective. His future goal would override his past performance. He had to transferr the energy he spent on the past to whatever it took to press toward the mark that God had set for Him. For Paul, that mark was to preach the gospel with all his might and to attain his place in the kingdom as a believer in Jesus Christ. His purpose was to empower others, to bring healing and meaning to the lives of others. He traveled from city to city and planted churches, trained leaders, and other pastors. He had suffered many challenges, but his life's goal was to focus on his calling and to comfort others with the same power of God that had comforted him. In other words, there is a bigger picture. The past, the loss, the pain, and sorrow are all just pieces of the big puzzle of life.

Now take a look at the big picture of your life and put things in the proper perspective. Keep in mind that the big picture of your life is not yet complete. Some puzzle pieces are missing. These puzzle pieces are your future.

I could somewhat relate to Paul as I made decisions that would affect my future. The picture wasn't complete. In looking back, my life included my husband and my role as a wife. That was the picture of yesterday. If I were to go into the studio for a photo shoot today, there would only be pictures of myself. Now, my future portrait could be different! However, as I continue to glance back and put the past in perspective, at the time, my first career was still that of a music teacher. However, this job was combined with my life as a wife. In the past, decisions were made in consideration of my husband and children. I realized that focusing too much on this perspective in life brought more sorrow and confusion as to what to do next. I did not need to include my husband in my future decisions. He was no longer here. Nothing I did would ever again affect his life. He was in the hands of God, living in his eternal home. That was beyond my control.

As I experienced various stages of grief, I took inventory of my job and how I would move forward with this. Not only did I enjoy teaching, I knew that I was a gifted teacher and a talented musician. I did not necessarily need professional evaluations to know that I was competent in my job. I considered teaching my passion and my calling. My students brought much comfort. I loved and appreciated my co-workers. I loved my school. However, I knew that my deepest passion and calling was in full-time ministry. God called me to preach the gospel.

My personal goal and passion was and still is to Encourage, Equip and to Empower others to fulfill their divine destiny and predestined purpose in life. My goal was and still is to use my resources and influence to enhance the quality of life for others. I began to look forward to what that might look like if I were to focus solely on this powerful passion and vision that God had placed in my soul. I prayed about my deepest desires and goals that had been in my heart and soul long before this event of loss had occurred. I decided to pursue this as soon as the opportunity presented itself. It was time. There was pain, although it was now less intense – but slowly the energy it took to grieve was swallowed up in planning my future and reaching my goals.

Looking forward is what it takes to move through and beyond the season of grief. I made the decision that I couldn't just let my life flow, and the chips fall where they may. I made a decision not to let my grief dictate what I would accomplish in a given day. I set goals and timelines that also included quiet time to think and take care of my emotions. I wrote down these goals, marked my calendar, and did research on what it would take to heal and fulfill God's purpose. Yes, I sustained a loss. But mourning would not define my life. Therefore, to press means to get up and travel down the road predetermined by God, even though the tears may fall. That's the only way you will ever move forward. Truthfully, I realized that if I still had the responsibilities as a wife, I would not have pursued some of these goals. However, God's timing for my life at this moment was that I would not have those obligations. That indeed is purpose!

PASSION, PURPOSE AND THE FUTURE

Music and teaching have always been my passion. But I envisioned many years before Raliegh's death that I would eventually attend seminary, pursue a career as an author, and avail myself to the ministry of motivational speaking, preaching and teaching at conferences, retreats, etc. While teaching full time, and pastoring full time, I decided to pursue a degree in theology. It took me two years to graduate with an M.A. in Theology with a 3.75 average. Before my last semester in school, the door opened for early retirement as a teacher. Of course, after much prayer, by faith, I retired. During my last semester, instead of pursuing yet another degree as I had planned, I prayed that God would open the door for me to start my writing career. I received a call the next week from a publisher who needed an author for a project. God opened the door for me to become the author of my first book, *"African American Daily Devotions 2014."* God opened doors for book signings and appearances on author panels, book fairs, and other events. And now, here I am publishing my second book, with two other projects already started and in the wings.

Also, I decided to get involved in my community on various Boards and leadership roles, as well as support my dearly beloved alma mater, Fisk University in any way that I can. We have also formalized a partnership with a network of churches in Liberia, West Africa and established an international ministry. Our church is the mother church, and I now serve as Overseer and sponsor of the Angela Roberts Jones Elementary School in Grand Bassa, Liberia West Africa.

In essence, I began to pursue the passions and dreams that had become dormant in a sense because, in the past, my life had been consumed by other responsibilities. My pain had now served as a jumpstart to the pursuit of other interests. Another chapter of my life was about to begin as my book of life would continue to be written. My dreams were becoming a reality. As long as you have breath in your body, you are writing the chapters of your life. Your deceased loved one would have wanted you to continue to pursue your dreams.

I can attest to the fact that the scripture found in Romans 8:28: "All things work together for the good of them who love God and are the called according to His purpose," is real and relevant to our lives today. In this particular verse, the word "purpose" can be defined as: "to set forth" or "a setting forth." It is something that God plans and puts into action because of His will. His will is described as His desire for the earth, for humanity, for you as an individual. You are here because God willed you to be here. Because of His desire, He has set in motion a plan for your life. A part of that plan included your loss and grief process. All of this works together for your good to bring about God's intended purpose for your life.

I came to Clarksville, or so I thought at the time, as a pastor's wife to help fulfill the purpose that was set forth with my husband who was called to pastor here. And secondly, I felt that I was called to be here as a helpmate as I too journeyed through my personal dreams and goals. However, he is gone, and I am the one who is still here. I am here because God planned for me to be here. His plans are perfect.

At the time, fulfilling my duty as a supportive wife and a helpmate was the means to an end of achieving God's purpose for my life. We all fill roles on earth. There are roles in our relationships, husband/wife, mother/father, brother or sister, co-worker, church member, friend, etc. Although I believe that God ordains relationships, the role you play in that relationship does not define who you are and your purpose for being on this earth. Relationships enhance, encourage and enlighten you along this journey. Some may beg to differ, but you were not birthed only to take on the identity of your mate. God gave your life, vision, gifts, a personality, and desires. Losing a spouse doesn't take away the core of who you are.

GOD'S PURPOSE OVERPOWERS PAIN

In my pursuit to gain an understanding of my life, God led me to read entries in some of my journals that I had written years ago. Several of my journals contained prayers, special events, the description of the emotions experienced during various events in my life and special revelations from God during those times. One day I was compelled to reflect on the confirmation of my calling into the ministry. Three distinct events remain etched in my memory. The first was a vision I had at a conference while the speaker was reading the sixth chapter of Isaiah. I remember being taken up in the spirit as if I left the room and was supernaurally transported into a chamber where Jesus lay on a slab with a sheet covering his entire body. As I approached Him, He got up from the slab and reached out to me. I distinctly remember the scenery and being in His presence. It was if He was letting me know that He would be with me as I moved forward to obey His instructions.

    I later experienced another vision on a separate occasion as I was sleeping. During this particular point in time, I was studying the book of Daniel at the time. I distinctly remember waking and rising in bed as if someone was pulling me up. It was an out of body experience that made me feel like I was out of this world. I was somewhat disoriented when my husband asked me what was wrong. I replied – "I just had a talk with Ezekiel the prophet." He was giving me clarity and instructions. I also remember saying as I awakened that I was talking to God. However, when I woke up, I realized that God was speaking to me through this experience and was leading me to study the Words of the prophet Ezekiel.

    In another event, I was also awakened in the middle of the night to get up and go to the living room. As I opened my Bible, the page immediately went to the Great Commission. As I sat there reading, I began to weep. It felt as if someone was standing over me turning the pages and reading the words on the page. I felt an unusual presence. In my spirit, I felt that this was the voice of Jesus Christ speaking directly to me. Now, someone reading this may think that I was hallucinating and may have an emotional disturbance. However, I know that anyone who has experienced the call of God, or the unique presence of God in the person of the Holy Spirit can somewhat relate to my experience. God has a way of individualizing his voice so that the intended listener knows who is speaking.

My answer to the call in ministry was very controversial. I was the first female minister licensed in my church. The denominational organization that our church was a part of during that time in the early nineties did not believe in women in ministry; therefore, we were voted out. The challenges I faced early in ministry helped to make my calling and divine encounters so clear and profound. Losing my husband and becoming the Senior Pastor was an added responsibility. Also, I became the first female pastor of our church. This experience caused me to search out my purpose and the plan for my life even more.

All of the visions and encounters that I just mentioned suddenly became relevant to this very moment in time. Here I was again not only grieving but in the middle of yet another question from others as to whether or not my call was legitimate. However, I had felt such a powerful presence of God through this grief process that any questions now about my calling were entirely irrelevant. I had experienced such deep sorrow at the loss of my husband that I came to the firm resolve that if this was meant to be, the battle was not mine, it was the Lord's. I could only focus on one day at a time. But as God would have it, my divine destiny was to become the Senior Pastor of our church. If it were up to me, I would have waited a little longer and taken more time to grieve. But that was not God's will.

What does this have to do with my grief and healing process, you may ask? Well, this very experience helped me to understand the importance of being obedient to God and moving forward. I began to feel more sensitive to the pain and challenges of others. There was work to do. There were people around me who needed me to step up in obedience. It was not about me per se, but about God's plan. The spiritual gifts God had placed in me became keener. I began to feel this incredible determination to empower people as never before. Although I had always felt this, I knew that at this moment in time, God had brought me to a definite crossroad in my life. This call – this passion – this revelation became so much stronger and powerful than my pain. Purpose was calling me. I had to move forward!

Furthermore, as I reflect or glance back on my childhood, I remember that my parents were very active in the community, and in the church. I saw my mother and father work as teachers, in ministry, and as leaders in our community. My brothers and sisters and I were a part of that, we witnessed that, and they poured into us as children. Everything that I needed to move forward from this challenging event in my life was instilled from the time of my birth. Your past may not be my past, but God uses everything in our lives, the good, bad, and the ugly to bring about the purpose He set forth before the beginning of time. His purpose is to be glorified and to bring salvation to man. His plan came through Jesus Christ, by the Holy Spirit. There is a power that works in us because Christ dwells in us. Through it all, we must learn to trust in God and depend on His Word, His Faithfulness, and His Power, which all ultimately works for His Purpose. Everything you experience in your life will work together for that end because you are a child of God.

PAIN MANAGEMENT

If you have ever suffered physical pain from an injury, you may recall that doctors prescribe a pain management plan so that one can function normal capacity. The goal is to manage the pain so that you can live a normal life and carry out a daily routine. Similarly, at the outset of the death of your loved one, you must determine that this will only be a season of mourning and not a lifetime of grief. Instead of allowing the pain to control you, make a decision that you will work through this so that grief does not define or derail your destiny. You have to take steps to manage the pain. This decision will affect your journey through this season. However, it is understood that the period of grief is a personal journey with elements varying from person to person.

Several factors affect the grief process. One is personality. Some people may face pain head on as indicative of their personality whereas others avoid facing pain and confronting obstacles. Some personalities are lighthearted and optimistic while others have a tendency to experience depression and doubt. Religious beliefs also play a significant part. There are some whose faith is firm. They believe and trust in God because they know that He will never leave nor forsake them. They believe in His plan because they know that ultimately, all will work out for good.

And then there is the relationship factor. Your grief process could be affected by dynamics of your relationship with the deceased. There are some who grieve with regret. Their sorrow seems to stem from the "could have," "would have," "should have" syndrome. These feelings magnify the grief process and can hinder the spirit of peace and comfort. On the contrary, there are some whose memories of the deceased are comforting and reflective of good times and positive events. I believe that healthy grieving includes both of these factors. At any rate, to grieve in a healthy manner, you must resolve at some point that there was nothing more you could have done, and most of all, there is nothing you can do now. What's done is done. Gaze – seek, set your heart on moving forward. Look forward, think forward, move forward.

A very fitting example of this very principle can be found in the story of David and the loss of his child in 2 Samuel 12:15-23. Verse 15 says that when David's child became ill, he fasted and prayed and even lay out on the ground all night. On the seventh day, the child died. According to the scripture, this death was something that God allowed to happen because of David's adultery with Bathsheba and the murder of her husband, Uriah. The servants were afraid to tell David that the child was dead because of the overwhelming grief that David had already displayed while the child was deathly ill. Nonetheless, they had to tell him the devastating news.

Surprisingly, they did not see the response that they expected. Instead, of the uncontrollable grief they anticipated, David got up from the ground, washed his face, changed his clothes and went to the house of God to worship. He then went home and instructed his servants to prepare food. The servants looked at him and thought David had lost his mind. David did not follow the traditional ritual of mourning, but instead, he got up and ate. They were dumbfounded. Verses 22-25 explain David's resolve and response to the servants. It reads:

> David replied, "I fasted and wept while the child was alive, for I said, 'Perhaps the Lord will be gracious to me and let the child live.' But why should I fast when he is dead? Can I bring him back again? I shall go to him, but he shall not return to me." Then David comforted Bathsheba; and when he slept with her, she conceived and gave birth to a son and named him Solomon. And the Lord loved the baby, and sent congratulations and blessings through Nathan the

prophet. David nicknamed the baby Jedidiah (meaning, "Beloved of Jehovah") because of the Lord's interest.

Yes, you guessed it! David and Bathsheba moved on from the pain of their sin and the loss of their child. As a result, God blessed them to have another child named Solomon. He became the next King of Israel and was known as the richest and wisest man of his time. Solomon, also known as the wise preacher is also the author of the books of Proverbs, Ecclesiastes and the Song of Solomon found in the Bible. The death of one child did not abort the purpose of the next child that was already set forth by God. The moral of the story is, don't cancel your future by refusing to move forward. David came to the resolve that he had done all he could do, so he purposely brought an end to his grieving.

MOVING FORWARD

- An essential element in walking in your purpose is to shift gears from surviving to thriving. You must eventually shift gears and stop grieving. You are not just a survivor of your spouse. You are an individual. You have a name. You have a reason to be still on this earth. If you don't know what that is, then take some time to find out. Don't just sit there and wait. Get up and make something happen. Life does not have to be the same. Rebuke the fears and embrace the future. Pray and ask God to open up your mind to new possibilities and new memories.
- Now is the time to take responsibility for your life. Your family and friends can cry with you, but ultimately no one can truly help you to move forward.
- Ponder on the following questions: "What can I do to promote my healing and progress? How can I improve the quality of my life?"
- You may want to tackle some of the unresolved issues between you and your deceased loved one. Glance back long enough to identify those negative feelings and seek healing.
- Journaling is a healthy way to express and expel thoughts, revelations, prayers, answers to prayers, etc. We have not because we ask not. Knowing where you have been will help you to envision

where you are going. God will undoubtedly reveal and open the pathways to allow you to look and move forward.

THE SUPPORT TEAM

- Avoid drilling the one you seek to encourage on the details of the past, the death event, their emotions, their challenges, etc. There are some that are concerned, but there are others that are just plain nosy. Please don't allow yourself to be in the category of those who are inappropriately inquisitive!
- The experienced and wise counselor and minister understand how to gently and safely guide the one grieving through a myriad of painful memories and guide them safely back to the present.
- Put the needs of the one you are seeking to encourage above your human curiosity.

FURTHER REFLECTION

Now is the time to make concrete plans on what you need to do to move past this time in your life. Read the following scriptures and record your thoughts: Proverbs 3:5-6, Romans 9:10-16, Philippians 3:12-14, James 1:5

SECTION THREE
THE STRENGTHENING PHASE

"You were given this life, because you
are strong enough to live it."
~Robin Sharma

And He said to me, "My grace is sufficient
for you, for My strength is made perfect in
weakness." Therefore most gladly I will rather
boast in my infirmities, that the power of
Christ may rest upon me. Therefore I take
pleasure in infirmities, in reproaches, in needs,
in persecutions, in distresses, for Christ's sake.
For when I am weak, then I am strong.
~2 Corinthians 12:9-10 (NKJV)

6

THE SHIFT...
From Marriage to Singleness

The end – but the beginning!
Seems like an oxymoron – but a profound truth.
~Angela Roberts Jones

Therefore, if anyone *is* in Christ, *he is* a new creation; old
things have passed away; behold, all things have become new.
~2 Corinthians 5:17

The third and final memorial service was held in E. St. Louis at Raliegh's home and birth church. Ironically, I had to walk down the aisle by myself behind the casket at the end of the service. The usual procedure for most funerals is to walk the spouse down the aisle or pair them with another family member so that they do not walk alone. As I followed the casket, I vividly recall thinking, "I have done this so many times" with Raliegh as Pastor and myself as Co-Pastor, and even in family processionals, "and here I am alone." I stood up straight, wiped my tears and walked tall and boldly down the aisle. I felt an unusual strength, a unique presence of comfort, peace and release to pick up the pieces and move forward. I can't explain it, but I knew that it would be alright and that I would do what I had to do.

This was the end, but the beginning. I had to walk this path alone, me and the Lord. It was divinely orchestrated that I would walk down the aile that day alone. It was an indication to me and all of those present that I was now widowed, unmarried, single. I was alone, but not forsaken by God. It would be tough to walk alone, but I had no choice. In my son's words, "these are the cards we had been dealt."

The stark reality that we were no longer one flesh and that I was without my husband set in at that moment. Living single is one thing. But being thrust into singleness with no warning was another matter.

ONE FLESH

Marriage is the most intimate relationship on earth. Paul uses the analogy of marriage in Ephesians 5:22-33 to illustrate the covenant relationship of Jesus Christ and the church. The scripture instructs the husband to love his wife as his own body, and the wife to submit to this love and respect her husband. Think about it, until you are married (ideally, but maybe not necessarily realistically in this day and time!) no one should see your body, or have access to the private chambers of your heart. To love your own body means to tend to its every need. The body needs food, rest and exercise to survive. But we also do the little extras of pampering our bodies to make ourselves comfortable like dressing nice, smelling sweet, visits to the nail and hair salon, and so on.

We realize that in marriage, our body is truly not just our own. However, the instruction to the husband to love the body of his wife is not just physical. He is also charged to nurture and protect her as she grows to become the woman God has purposed her to be. Likewise, the woman is a helper to her husband as he strives to live out his purpose here on earth. We must share our entire life – to some degree. Sharing in marriage has its benefits. For one, when a man loves a woman, he does his best to take care of her. Therefore, she feels secure. When a woman loves a man, she doesn't mind pampering him and holding him in high esteem. Submission is not an issue when a man truly loves a woman. Wow! Imagine losing that!

Traditionally, the woman takes on the last name of the husband. The whole world identifies her, as in my case, Mrs. Jones. Her identity has blended into his identity. She is no longer identified solely by the name that her family and friends knew her. Furthermore, the married woman (or man) has a companion to attend to her needs, to be a companion for the journey of life, and vice versa for the man. Because of this, it is possible to lose sight of your individualism and sense of independence because of the blending of life and purpose with your mate. In essence, you live in partnership with your mate. However, that's not a bad thing because the two become one flesh. Becoming one flesh is what God intended for marriage.

As I grieved, I could literally feel the severing of two lives that had become one flesh. Not only was there a heartfelt emotional pain, but I experienced physical ache deep in my chest. One day I walked into my den, and I felt as if my very right side was being ripped off. I fell to me knees in a painful cry and just stayed there until it subsided. I was home alone at the time. It was difficult to talk about this publicly. In my case, everyone I met was so grieved over the loss of *their* friend, pastor, community leader, mentor, brother, uncle, father, or whatever relationship they claimed, that they all forgot that I was still here, or so it felt. Living in a glass bowl is not easy when you are grieving. But anyway, who would understand this or even believe this? There was some concern displayed for my well-being by many. But it was difficult to explain this to someone who had never experienced this.

EMBRACING SINGLENESS

Shifting from marriage to singleness....this is what I faced. To be single simply means to journey through life or a season in your life without a spouse. It's as simple as that. But it's not so simple when you have to adjust from mariage to being single after experiencing marriage for some years. However, the adjustment can and must be made. I discovered that being single is more of a mindset than just your social status. The life of the single individual focuses on fulfilling your personal needs, goals and desires without having the added responsibility or privilege of considering someone else.

There are degrees of singleness, the single mother or father, the one divorced, the one who never married, and, of course, the widow. Society has a tendency to lump all singles together. But you can't judge a book by its cover. You must understand the backstory to understand the person. However, no one else may know your story, but you know it. The way you embrace being single depends on how you see yourself. If your attitude is positive, it may take some time, but you will embrace this season as ordained by God. After all, "the Lord giveth and the Lord taketh away. Blessed be the name of the Lord." (Job 1:21). If your thoughts are pessimistic, you will miss the purpose and meaning of this particular season in your life and continue to grieve over your loss.

Some people do not feel that they are a whole person without a spouse. That may be possible to an extent, but where and when did you adopt that attitude? We sometimes allow the world to define and categorize us socially. I do believe that everybody needs somebody. But this doesn't mean that everyone will be married. Truthfully, I enjoyed marriage. But does being married or even being single define who you are deep on the inside? Who are you really and what does God have to say about it? As a matter of fact, you were born into this world by yourself, and this is the way you will leave.

It took a little time for me to become comfortable with being single. My mind and heart were trained to consider my mate. But I began to understand and embrace the blessing of being single. It didn't happen overnight. There were a few steps to this process to conducting life as a single individual. First of all, my husband's name was on almost everything. I had to present the death certificate to do business and remove his name from the accounts. You just don't realize how much your life is entangled as a married couple until separation occurs, either through death or for some, divorce.

As a matter of fact, after seven years, I still had to present the death certificate just the other day to conduct some personal business. However, initially, this process took longer than I anticipated because it was emotionally traumatizing. This responsibility magnified the tearing apart of the one flesh of marriage. The process included paying bills, completing financial aid papers for my kids to stay in college, mortgage, house repairs, automobile concerns, survivor rights and responsibilities, and so on.

It took a few years for me to unravel all of this. But I did it. I immediately took control of my life, one day at a time, one step at a time. I recall telling my children one day that I was single. My son threw up his hand and put it on his head and said, "Mom don't say that." Of course at the time, he could still see Mom and Dad in his mind, and not just Mom. Not only did my family have to accept the fact that I was entirely responsible for my affairs, but also embrace the fact that I was capable and okay because God was with me. I didn't ask for this. I had faith in the power of God that if He brought me to this, He would take me through it!

And then, there was the issue of attending public and family events alone with no escort or companion. I found it awkward, lonely, and sometimes embarrassing at times because there were people that would look at me with pity, or make statements like, "I know you miss your husband." How was I supposed to answer this? I learned to answer just as I was feeling, "Of course I do, but I am okay with this. God's got it!" I was aware that some people just don't know what to say. I had to encourage others to embrace my singleness and the fact that this is just how it is. I decided to reach down into myself to unleash my life's purpose and passions. I had to become comfortable with myself and enjoy doing things alone.

I revisited the promises God had made to me. I decided to travel and pursue and rekindle relationships with friends and family. It was important to reach out and accept relationships with people who embraced my singleness as well. I did not need to be around people who consistently reminded me that I did not have a mate. A few of the relationships that I had with people as a married woman eventually faded, because I discovered that some of the people we knew as a couple were only connected to my husband, or to the union of my husband and I, and not to me as an individual. Many married couples do not feel comfortable with developing relationships socially with single individuals. However, I did not experience this until I became single.

One of the key factors to embracing singleness is to establish a support system for people who can empathize and relate to where you are in life. Although I value my relationships with some married couples, I began to realize that singles need to support each other. This became a stark reality as I attended various events as the only, or one of the only single people in the group. For example, I recall going to dinner with several ministry couples. Provisions for seating were made, and as an afterthought, they had to pull up a chair and find somewhere for me to sit. I discovered that singles sometimes get stuck off on the backside of a table, on the far side of the room (in many cases) and sometimes with the children. There are also times when singles end up being the babysitter during events instead of socializing and enjoying adult conversation, which is needed for unmarried adults just as for married adults.

I have also participated in various events where couples have an escort because they have each other. Usually, if I didn't bring anyone with me, someone had to be found to walk with me or keep me company. This was also very uncomfortable at times. I eventually had to insist that I was okay. I'm single. There's nothing wrong with not having an escort! All of this was a huge adjustment to my social status. Social status only identifies how you relate to people and how they relate and interact with you. I quickly saw that being single was far different at my age than it was when I was in college and at the age of my twenties. At my age, most people have been married for years with children, and even grandchildren, mortgages and a ton of other responsibilities. This was different! I could write another book on just this subject.

Moving from marriage to being single also brought a challenge of my new found singleness when conducting business with people who insisted on going down memory lane of my husband, and their reflections on various events. I soon learned that I needed to make new relationships and reclaim my friends and life, even to the point of my business relationships. If I had not done that, I never could have moved away from grief. Even until this day, there are still people that I cannot carry on a conversation with because their memory of my late husband dominates. My children said to me one day, "Mom, I can't take this emotional roller coaster today!" In other words, they were referring to the fact that we would have to sit in yet another program where someone felt that they had to go down memory lane to remember their dear friend (my husband and their father). I appreciate the memory and the love that many had for him, but there were times that I was living so in the moment that I would just be caught off guard by going down memory lane, especially after several years have passed. But, I survived! I learned how to gently make the conversation more relevant to the here and now.

TAKING OFF THE WEDDING RING

Another challenge through this process was for me to take off my wedding ring. I continued to faithfully wear my wedding ring for close to a year. I would get up in the morning and put it on as usual. But one morning, I felt the unction after putting it on, to take it off. I tried, but as I removed it, I couldn't fight the tears, so I put it back on. This went on for about a week. Then finally, I took it off and did not try to camouflage by putting on another ring. Truthfully, I felt almost naked and even very uncomfortable with not wearing my wedding ring. Taking off the rig an admission to the whole world that I was single, my husband was not here and would never come back. Even more importantly, it was a huge emotional step to accept the fact that he was gone and would never come back.

To those who knew me, it was obvious that I had come to the point of emotional healing that I was eternally separated from my husband forever. Taking off the ring permanently was painful and awkward. But this process was a part of my shift from pain to purpose. There was purpose even in my being single for such a time as this.

People were watching me as I went through these stages of acceptance, which was also extremely uncomfortable for me. My pain was my pain. My struggle was my struggle. I appreciated the prayers and the support, but many people on the outside could only speculate about what was truly going on in my world. For example, I was out of town for a ministry engagement. My host knew my husband and knew us as a couple. At dinner, one particular day, one of the other guest made the comment that they noticed that I no longer wore my wedding ring. They further commented that I must be looking for a boyfriend. Well, I responded by saying, "I might be." However in my heart, I reflected on the pain of taking off the ring. The comment was not meant to be harmful, but it stirred up the memory of the struggle in me as I finally accepted the fact that I was alone in this world without my mate. This comment was insensitive and presumptuous. You would think that they would consider the fact that here was a woman whose husband died. I wasn't single by choice. Taking off the ring was a sensitive subject. Especially for someone who barely even knew me.

However, I understand that most people don't think when they speak, and they don't mean any harm. But nonetheless, you must understand, singleness to me did not mean that I wasn't married. It merely meant that my husband died. The thought process for these two categories of being single is entirely different. I had to come to grips with being single and change my approach to my lifestyle. The ring had to come off and stay off.

Angela Roberts Jones

LIVING SINGLE

Another challenge to singleness was the adjustment to living alone. Not only was the bed cold, but the whole house also seemed extra cold during the winter time. One of my high school friends and I joked about this. He was also a widower, so he understood this experience. It was sad, but it was funny. It was comforting to know that someone else was also going through this! Living alone also entailed hearing noises in the house because the house was too quiet. It included now moving from room to room without any interference.

However, in time, this too became a blessing. I began to enjoy and embrace my quiet time. This was my space, and I could do absolutely anything I felt like without being distracted. I live in every room of my home. It is furnished to my liking, although I am still working on it. I don't have to share closets. I clean up when I feel like it. I come and go as I please without being accountable to anyone. I am free to write, meditate and pray, study my scriptures, play the piano, sing and even talk on the phone whenever I feel like it. I go to bed when I feel like it, get up when I am ready, and eat when I feel like it, and cook if or when I feel like it. This new found freedom opened the door for my involvement in things that I enjoy. What was once a burden had become a blessing!

SINGLENESS IS NOT A CURSE. It took some time for me to come to a peaceful resolve with my new status in life, but I did. I determined that my loss would not cripple my ability to be at peace with myself or the world around me. It is a proven fact that you cannot embrace your life and move forward if your thoughts are consumd by self-pity. Furthermore, it can be challenging to embrace singleness if those around you have a difficult time seeing you as an individual. There were some people I encountered who stated to me that whenever they saw me, they saw my husband. They could not embrace me as an individual because they were accumstomed to seeing my husband and me together. They could only see the married me with something missing.

I began to realize that this was part of their grief process and the adjustments they had to make. Not only did I have to adjust to being single, my family, friends, and acquaintances had to make the same adjustment. Because of these encounters, I was motivated to purposely and intentionally determine that this was a time of rediscovery and recovery for me as an individual. That meant understanding that I had to separate my grief issues from the grief issues of others, including my children. Grief is a personal journey of acceptance, adjustments and healing. I decided that I could not take on the responsibility of someone else's adjustment process. That burden was too much to bear. We should not project our grief on others, nor should we allow others to project their pain on us, although it is human and very easy to do. This revelation brought freedom and healing to my heart.

To embrace singleness means to become one with yourself and your God-given purpose. Not in a selfish way, but in a way that you are secure in who you are and the place God has allowed you to be at this particular point in time. I learned to love my new life. I love to drive and travel to different places. I love people. I am passionate about reading and writing. I am passionate about ministry and empowering others, laughing and having fun. I am intelligent, creative, educated, gifted, anointed and full of vision and purpose. I am a teacher, leader, mentor, and friend. I have compassion and love for people. Being single meant that it was now my turn to explore life. And that's what I did, and I am still doing. I had worked hard all of my adult life to be a good wife and mother. When I lost my mate, it momentarily felt almost like God took my life away. It wasn't easy, but step by step, day by day, God's purpose for this single lady began to unfold. I had to reclaim my life and purpose and reset my priorities. Praise God for His peace and comfort.

In essence, He gave me new life. He was doing a new thing in me. Being single allowed me to embrace that new thing. I didn't exactly agree with losing my husband. Did I still grieve, yes of course I did, but for only a season. The grief was not only for the loss of my husband but for the loss of what my life had been as a wife and the future life I had anticipated with my husband. I had to change my plans. This is all a part of the normal grief process. As the seasons of my life changed, determination, enthusiasm, and positive expectations to receive what God had for me in this phase of my life became exciting. I began to look forward to the possibility of getting married again, to seeing the world, a new career and making new friends. I started to see the world as an adventure waiting to be explored. There were places I had not been, people I had not met, and things I had not done. Being single would allow me to do some of the things I could not do while married. That is simply the real truth. The shift from pain to purpose, marriage to singleness was all in God's hands!

MOVING FORWARD

- Build a support team of individuals who accept you as a single person with life and purpose, and are interested in your personal pursuits.
- The reality is that you are now single, and a new mindset must take place. Therefore, this support group is not your cry group, but your moving forward group who you can indulge in conversation and activities without reminding you of the loss of your mate. This group will encourage you to explore, to live, to make new friends and see life as an adventure.

THE SUPPORT TEAM

- Let me invite you to pray and ask God to help you see the mourning individual as an individual. Take time to listen to their life and events that occurred before meeting their spouse. The conversation should now focus on the person, and not their loss. Help them to deal with reality and view life in the present time.
- Avoid looking upon the one grieving with pity. Take the time to develop a healthy attitude about the life of living single.
- Treat the now single individual with the same dignity and consideration as that of a married person.
- Help the one grieving to search out activities and events conducive for single living.

FURTHER REFLECTION

Read books and testimonies that are encouraging and positive of single successful individuals, most especially if they have lost a spouse. Read the following scriptures and record your thoughts: 1 Corinthians 7, Philippians 1:6, Ephesians 1:11

7

A NEW BEGINNING
Letting Go of the Old

"One of the most courageous decisions you'll ever make is to finally let go of what's hurting your heart and soul."
~Bridgette Nicole

Make up your mind that you will move forward. All things are possible with God. You can let go of the pain and the past.
~Angela Roberts Jones

"Do not remember the former things, nor consider the things of old. Behold, I will do a new thing, Now it shall spring forth."
~Isaiah 43:18-19b (NKJV)

It is tough to let go of a loved one who passes away, but at some point, you must. Some people are simply afraid to let go and move forward for various reasons. But I must emphatically state this to you: DON'T FEEL GUILTY ABOUT MOVING FORWARD! This may seem like a simple statement, but it is profound. Consider the fact that everyone else around you will move on, so you might as well do the same.

Angela Roberts Jones

LET GO

Eventually, the food, the calls, the visits, and the concern from others for your grieving will stop. People will move on with their lives and leave you sitting in the house crying. And frankly, that's okay. We all need to move forward in search of peace and happiness. You can't expect them to sit and hold your hand every day. You only have one life to live; you might as well enjoy it while you can. The decision to move forward is crucial to your journey of overcoming the pain. This decision will cause your life to shift from a pain and survival mode to a thriving, happiness and living out your purpose mode. The strength to move forward starts first with your decision to let go of whatever may hinder you from progressing.

Furthermore, you should feel safe and confident that moving forward in your life is what God intended. You have to do whatever it takes and whatever works for you. The people around you may not understand or even agree with the choices you deem necessary to move forward. But ultimately, it's your decision. Moving forward involves deliberate and intentional actions. No one can live your life but you.

Filling your life with positive experiences will cause you to let go of the things that make you sad. I have to admit that this can be a real struggle. At some point, you must let go of certain memories and even items which constantly remind you of your loss. Items such as pictures, clothes, jewelry, furniture, books, or anything that might have belonged to your loved one, all have the potential to send you on a roller coaster of emotions. The question is, when and how do you let go and what do you let go of?

I tend to agree with therapist and counselors who advise the ones grieving not to make major decisions too soon after the trauma of the death of a loved one. You may later regret getting rid of something that could prove to be a blessing to you or others. It is better to wait until your head is clear before you make decisions even about your career, finances, your home, and other aspects that can permanently affect your life. Some decisions can cause deep regret and cannot reverse. Your flesh and emotions can lead you to do some strange things!

Some people build shrines to their loved ones. However, from my observation of my personal relationships, and as a pastor and spiritual counselor, and life coach, the people who do this struggle with personal happiness and guilt. These shrines, which consist of pictures, clothes, rooms that they never touch or change because it helps to keep their loved one alive, consistently frequent visits to the cemetery, and so on, tend to cause a perpetual up and down state of sadness and guilt. They never really let go so they never actually heal. The grief event seems to go on and on indefinitely. There are constant posts on social media and other memorial pages, request for prayer for their year- end year out sadness. It never stops! Consider the fact that museums are built to preserve history, artifacts, artwork, and so on. In a similar way, personal shrines with articles of our loved ones are meant to preserve not just their memory, but the moments in which they were alive. Preserving moments in time can also preserve the emotional trauma that comes with it. How do you move forward if you are working to stay reminded of memories and the emotions that pair with it? You must be mindful of what memories you are preserving. That's why it's important to let go of what makes you sad.

I must personally admit that letting go is much easier said than done. I remember making a decision to remove some of my husband's clothing and clean out a drawer. Before I could even start, I became extremely overwhelmed with grief. This process triggered the feeling of loss and the reality that he was never coming back. I realized that on my first attempt, I wasn't ready to do this. So I stopped in my tracks and decided to do it on another day. My opinion is that there is no set time for this event to occur. The timing is different for everyone. But at some point, you must make a decision on what to do with the personal items of your loved one. I know of several people who had someone else to come in and completely clean out the closets, drawers, and so on immediately because the sight of their loved one's belongings caused unbearable sorrow.

For some, the presence of the belongings of their loved one brings comfort. Therefore, I am not recommending that you should discard every single thing that belonged to your deceased loved one, nor should you destroy all of the pictures. At some point, some of these personal belongings will also bring about fond memories of happy times with your mate. Keeping select items bring balance to the process of grief and the journey to healing. The key is to monitor your emotions so that the presence of these belongings does not trigger a perpetual state of grief and sorrow that comes from living in the past. In essence, you must let go of that which hinders your healing, but cling to the precious memories, pictures or select objects.

One way to distinguish this is to take charge of your thoughts. Reflect on what you most enjoyed about marriage, the love and intimacy you shared, the things you loved and adored about your spouse, the birth of your children and significant events with them, milestones and accomplishments, great vacations and family events, and the list goes on and on.

After journeying through this grief and healing process for the past seven years, I have reached the conclusion that memories are going to come with or without turning your house or any room into a museum. There are special treasures that should not be discarded, but should be preserved to pass down to your children, and other family members. You cannot completely erase a person's life just because of grief and sadness. Sometimes, it's best to pack up some items in a box until your emotions have settled so that you have a clear head on what to do with them.

As the healing process develops, memories may bring certain emotions, but eventually, the grief and intense sorrow dissipates. You must have the courage to let go and let God heal. The Spirit of God will guide you through this process. God created you. He knows your heart better than you do. He will reveal the things that you should discard, and what you should keep. Will you choose the path of continued mourning or the road to happiness? Making a decision will cause a shift from mourning to happiness. What will it be? You can't do both!

DATING, COURTSHIP, REMARRIAGE

Many people associate moving forward after losing a mate with remarriage. The assumption of many is that if a widowed person does not remarry, they have a hard time moving forward. *Recovering socially and pursuing happiness does not necessarily mean that remarriage is the answer.* Remarriage depends on you as a person, your vision and plans, and God's will for your life. But indeed, because God honors the institution of marriage, then remarriage after becoming widowed is also honorable before God. I would venture to say that the widowed person who had a good marriage, and appreciates the institution of marriage would consider remarriage at some point. If you have any question concerning remarriage after becoming a widow, consider the following scripture:

> Now, dear brothers and sisters—you who are familiar with the law—don't you know that the law applies only while a person is living? For example, when a woman marries, the law binds her to her husband as long as he is alive. But if he dies, the laws of marriage no longer apply to her. So while her husband is alive, she would be committing adultery if she married another man. But if her husband dies, she is free from that law and does not commit adultery when she remarries. Romans 7:1-3 (NLT)

In other words, the widow is no longer legally bound to her deceased mate. It takes time to emotionally separate from your deceased mate, but inevitably, healing will come. I believe the best approach to new relationships of the opposite sex is not to look for a mate, but become comfortable as a single person and enjoy healthy friendships. Learning first how to be a companion to yourself is an excellent foundation before moving forward in a serious relationship. The thought of dating and courtship can also be intimidating. If you were married for some years, being single and meeting someone else can be extremely awkward.

Nevertheless, dating, courtship, and remarriage are all three different types of relationships. Dating can be described as going out to dinner, movies or sharing other activities with a friend or multiple friends. There is nothing wrong with dating if that is what you choose; however, there is no end to this type of dating in my opinion. There is the concern of avoiding emotional attachment and life commitment. Many people make the mistake of setting very high expectations from dating. Some people date with courtship and marriage in mind while others just desire someone to talk to or accompany them to activities or events. Some people look for others to help them out with daily tasks and situations. Dating is different for different people, which is why the expectations of the relationship should be discussed from the very beginning and as the relationship progresses. However, I believe that God has set all things in order, and all things will happen in His timing.

Learning to make friends of the opposite sex can be very rewarding. I am a living witness to that. It has been very healthy for me to have friends of the opposite sex who are just friends, who respect me as a person. It is also a blessing to have these same friends appreciate my relationship with God and my intent on moving forward with His calling and purpose. This same attitude is required of me as I honor and respect those God has placed in my life.

On the other hand, there is another purpose for courtship. The end goal of the relationship is usually marriage. You might say that courtship is dating with a purpose. The time spent together is quality time getting to know someone that you are interested in spending time for the rest of your life. These expectations should be communicated from the start of the relationship and regularly as the relationship progresses. I believe that those who are widowed need also to discuss specifics of your healing progress and accept the fact that this person will not be the same as your deceased spouse. Widows (widowers) automatically bring baggage to the table (as well as those who have been married and divorced). Let me remind you of chapter one and its description of the brokenness of the soul from the traumatic death event.

I thoroughly believe that marriage is much happier when each person is at peace with themselves. A person at peace brings peace to the relationship. Many people remarry soon after the death of their mate and later regret it. This decision can be detrimental to the relationship for the mere fact that you may not have had the opportunity to grieve properly, and evaluate your emotions, or a game plan for moving forward with life. Grief issues can potentially cloud your judgment, so remarriage is not to be taken likely. Before remarriage, consider the following:

- Do you understand yourself? Are you afraid of being lonely or spending the rest of your life by yourself?
- Do you understand and appreciate the audience of one, that is, you alone and your relationship with God?
- Who are you really without a mate?
- How has this traumatic experience affected your perspective on life?
- Are you steady and stable in your emotions and decision-making abilities? Is your personal business in order?

- Are you healed from this experience to the point that you can accept someone else in your life?
- Why do you want to remarry? Are you in love? Or do you just need someone to help you cook, clean, take care of the kids, your personal business, and so on? Be real about it!
- Are you marrying out of loneliness or grief, or do you sincerely feel that God has ordained this union?
- Have you shared necessary information about your life and your personal concerns with your potential mate?
- What is your financial status, and that of your potential mate? How will you manage finances as a couple?
- What are the status of you and potential mate's children?
- How will you deal with a blended family, even if there are grown children? Don't forget about the possibility of grandchildren. Can they come to visit? Can other family members visit?
- Where will you live, and who will pay the mortgage? Is living separately a possibility or probability?
- What is your goal and purpose in life? Is the goal and purpose in the life of your potential mate the opposite of yours, or do you both complement and enhance each other?
- What is your philosophy of marriage?
- What are some of the background experiences and issues of your potential mate?
- Do you know your potential mate, the good, bad and the ugly? As sure as there is a good side, there is a dark side.
- Are you being influenced to remarry because of outside pressures or inward convictions?
- Do you and your potential mate share love, respect, and appreciation for one another?
- How do you feel about sex, romance, and intimacy?
- What are your religious/spiritual convictions? ...and that of your future mate? Do you attend church? Is this important to you in your future marriage?

These are just a few questions that must be addressed within yourself and with your potential mate. You may not be able to give detailed answers to every single question right away, but at least, take it to God in prayer for the confirmation and clarity to move forward. Some things should be worked out before marriage, but there are also some things that God leads you to work through after marriage. It depends on you and your potential mate and your ability to communicate effectively to each other.

Also, your position and station in life, along with your values and beliefs dictate to an extent your actions and how you proceed in this area of your life. It is best to make a decision and stand by your convictions as one who is decisive and proactive rather than emotional and reactive before entering into a new relationship. Keep in mind that this is your life. God has a purpose for you. Everything you do will inevitably affect the realm of God's purpose for your life and even the life of your potential mate.

DON'T BE AFRAID TO TRY

You may be asking at this point if I have a personal testimony in this area. Well, I do realize that inquiring minds want to know! Several months before his death, Raliegh asked me if I would ever remarry if something happened to him. He had asked me this several times over the years, but this time, the conversation was serious. He was persistent in asking questions and insisted that I respond. "No, I seriously doubt it," was my reply. He asked why. I explained to him that I could not see myself starting over with another person. It took too much work to achieve what we had in our marriage, not just things, but life in general, the kids, getting to know each other, and so on. I could not see myself going through this same process again.

I jokingly said to him, "I can't see training someone else!" He looked at me and stated in a serious tone, "Girl, you better move on with your life. You can't grieve forever." He insisted that I remarry if something happened to him. Honestly, I was a little surprised by these conversations and truthfully a little disturbed. I was living in the present. I didn't anticipate him leaving this earth anytime soon. *(For those who may be tempted to take this literally, I don't believe in training a man! I believe in the biblical model of marriage as I explained in the previous chapter. God does the training; the husband and wife should just step out on faith and submit to God, and he will define the roles of husband and wife for each couple.)*

Immediately after becoming widowed, the thought of dating, courting and remarriage were the last thing on my mind. The idea of being in close relationship with someone else was a little repulsive. It took quite a while for me to consider the idea of a new relationship. I could not fathom joining with another man in holy matrimony. Many people asked me if I would ever remarry. I avoided the topic as long as I could. Believe it or not, this topic is difficult to discuss for someone who is widowed. I wasn't single by choice. My husband died, so I had to figure it all out, just me and the LORD!

As years passed, I began to hear God speak to me about remarriage. I remember saying to God, well if this is so, you will have to send him to me. In essence, I prayed that if this were the will of God, my future mate would have to find me and see me as his wife. I made the decision that moment that I did not want to date as the world defines dating. I didn't like the idea of having a friend this month, and then months down the road having another friend. Dating can lead to an emotional rollercoaster whether you are widowed, single, or whatever. As a woman of God in my position and a faith walker, I prayed to God and surrendered this to Him because He was the one who put it in my spirit. I recalled the conversations that my husband and I had concerning this, so I felt that when and if the time came, I would be alright. The apprehensiveness and fear began to disappear gradually as I continued to pray and allow the presence of God to heal my heart.

Then one day a new chapter began in my life. I was attending an event and was introduced to a friend of a friend. He had also lost his spouse just a few years back. That was already something major that we had in common. Some months later, he gave me a call, and some months later we decided to date. From the start of our relationship, we made a decision that we would court with the intention of marriage. Our meeting fell in line with what I had prayed and surrendered to God concerning meeting a future mate. According to our discussions, he felt the same in meeting me. I asked his thoughts on me including this testimony in my book. He said why yes. Mainly because we are in agreement that God ordained that we meet. He said to me on our first date that "he who finds a wife, finds a good thing." However, on the first date, we decided to trust God for the outcome.

As God began to deal with him on marriage, he decided not to look for a wife, but to allow God to lead him to his future wife. He also explained to me that he wasn't into this dating thing and that he believed in the institution of marriage. After meeting me that first time and praying for several months, he stated that he felt that God was leading him to pursue me as his future mate. He also said that this was important to him because he approached me and not the other way around. I appreciated this because this is what I prayed.

A few months back, I attended a luncheon with a group of ladies and the subject of the possibility of me remarrying came up. I was a little hesitant, but with some prompting by our host who already knew about my situation, I shared my experience. I had already shared that I was writing this book. They insisted that I include this testimony of my meeting my potential husband to be after experiencing the trauma of losing my mate. After fervent prayer I decided that they were right. As of now, it has not worked out as we planned. We have faced some challenges that only God can work out. Through this experience, I have learned to trust God's will and His timing.

I have counseled many others on the fact that dating in your forties and fifties is much different than dating in your twenties and thirties. The older you become, the more comfortable you become with a certain way of life. Making adjustments are not as easy to make. There is more to let go of after two people have lived and collected a myriad of experiences. These adjustments are compounded with the issues surrounding widowhood. We both found out that it's not as easy as we thought, but we trust God for His intended outcome.

You may be asking, "Why write about this experience?" I had a conversation with my mother about taking this entire section out because I felt that I could not honestly give a definite outcome by the time this book is published. Truthfully, I wanted to avoid the "want to know" inquiries! She encouraged me to leave it in. As I sought God for confirmation and remembered the conversation and encouragement of my potential mate, I was convinced through the leading of the Holy Spirit to leave it in. I know beyond a shadow of a doubt that my testimony is a blessing to someone else.

I have met some widowed people who later regret that they passed up the opportunity to remarry. It is my belief that those who read this will be inspired to renounce fear and allow yourself to at least try if God brings the opportunity your way. Never say never! My position now is "not my will Oh Lord, but thy will be done." Take one step at a time, one day at a time, and ignore opinions that may be contrary to what God has spoken for you at this stage in your life. Those who have not walked in these shoes have absolutely no idea of what it takes for someone widowed to move forward into a new relationship.

However, continuing on a personal note, this relationship has blessed me in many ways. I know that it is a blessing for someone to read this. Not only did I find companionship and someone to listen and share things with, but I also learned to open up to all of God's possibilities in my life. Relationships are also tied to God's purpose for our lives. Some people are in your life for a reason in that season. God has ordained some relationships to bring healing, enjoyment, personal growth and exposure to new possibilities. Some produce positive results, and some negative. Some relationships bring love, and some bring discipline and valuable lessons. If you listen to God and trust Him, you will find that very valuable lessons are to be learned that may not necessarily lead to marriage. In my case, I know that this relationship helped me to deal with many issues surrounding widowhood and the adjustment to my new life. I have been transformed by taking the time to move beyond my comfort zone to get to know someone else.

I eventually realized that the experience of being present when my husband died affected me in more ways than I could measure at the time. For a person who has experienced the personal trauma of trusting God but still losing my mate after praying and crying out, this lesson of allowing myself to trust someone else is huge and crucial to my well-being and moving forward. I know beyond a shadow of a doubt that God ordained our meeting. The lessons I learned through this relationship have been very positive, and have proven to be a catalyst to my moving forward. Iron sharpens iron! My mind for business and ministry have been sharpened. I have been motivated to embrace positively the future, to be patient, to release subconscious expectations and take a risk on being vulnerable to live. This calm resolve comes by trusting God for the outcome.

I also learned to appreciate every step of my journey in all aspects of my life because it works together to fulfill God's ultimate plan. At this moment, I am very thankful to God for guiding my footsteps through all of this. I made the choice years ago that I would lay down my garments of mourning so that God could clothe me with His love and comfort, His peace and purpose. I encourage you to do the same. Be positive in your assessment of judgment of relationship possibilities. Give the person the benefit of the doubt, be patient, prayerful, purposeful and positive. Search God for his promises. However, by all means, learn how to enjoy the moment. It may feel awkward, but don't be afraid to try. You just might miss your blessing!

I will always honor my late husband, but I am especially grateful that he insisted on having the conversation about remarriage. Believe it or not, this very discussion helped to ease the pain and free my heart so that I could move forward. In fact, when you have experienced a good marriage, the prospect of remarriage doesn't sound like a bad idea. God knew far ahead that you would be in this season, and He knows about tomorrow. There are some things that we attempt to force into existence, but I don't believe that remarriage should be one of them. God is the one who opens and closes the doors to relationships. When God sends the right person, it will all work out in God's appointed time!

BE THANKFUL

I would say that the first thing to be thankful for is the life of your deceased loved one. The central focus of grief is to sorrow over the loss of your loved one. However, you can shift your thinking from focusing on the fact that you lost them to the fact that you are grateful to God for allowing them to be in your life. Strength comes when you shift from pain to praise. Praise God for what you had, but praise God that you are still here to live this life. Thank God for the opportunity to do some new things and make some new memories.

I mentioned earlier in this chapter that I traveled to Key West, Florida on vacation. This was a time for me to be alone and reflect the impact of my loss. This time away gave me the opportunity to seek God for direction on how to reset my life. One day as I was walking on the beach, I came upon a walkway that had anonymous quotes printed on it. One of those quotes read: "It is better to have loved and lost than never to have loved at all (Alfred Lolyd Tennyson)." I refer to this as my defining moment because of the significant shift that took place in my heart.

It was at this point that I began to give God praise for twenty-five years of marriage. I had not only grieved over the loss of my husband, but also over the fact that we were planning to renew our vows for our twenty-fifth wedding anniversary, but he did not live to see it. I thanked God for blessing us with beautiful children, and for allowing us to live together and work together in ministry. I began to focus on all of the good things that I experienced while married.

For example, we would sit up late at night and just laugh about what we experienced during the day. As I sat on the beach, so many things came to mind on why I should be thankful. I also had children waiting back at home for me. What if I didn't have them? My heart was filled with praise and worship to God for the gift that He had blessed me with, but had taken away. I couldn't wait to get back to the hotel and write down all of my many blessings and for the life, I shared with my husband. I had now shifted from grieving over his death and the issues surrounding the death event to thanking God for his life, our life together, and my future.

I Thessalonians 5:16-18 (NLT) says: "Always be joyful. Never stop praying. Be thankful in all circumstances, for this is God's will for you who belong to Christ Jesus." This verse was written to the believers in Thessalonica to advise them of the attitude they should possess in the midst of suffering and very challenging circumstances. The scripture does not say to be necessarily thankful for a particular affliction, but to be grateful in the middle of it. This is easier said than done when you are hurting. But it can be done. If you take inventory of your life, and the circumstances surrounding you, be intentional in counting your blessings. You will realize that your circumstances could be much worse. On a personal note, this particular scripture became alive to me as I sat on the beach at the sunset of that beautiful day! Thank God for the Holy Spirit. He gives us peace as He speaks in the middle of the storms of life.

It is my personal experience and observation that the attitude and belief system that you possess before going into a crisis affects your ability to have a heart of gratitude. If you are a person of faith, then your faith will prevail through the tears. The person who fosters a negative attitude rooted in self-pity, self-centeredness, anger and bitterness, this view will prevail and pose a threat to full healing. Your perspective of death also affects your ability to have an attitude of gratitude.

The scripture found in 1 Thessalonians 4:13 says that we are not to mourn as one with no hope. The following verse (14) says: "For since we believe that Jesus died and was raised to life again, we also believe that when Jesus returns, God will bring back with him the believers who have died." This verse explains why Christians should not grieve in the same manner as one who has no relationship with God. We believe that those who die in the Lord go to heaven. If we are faithful to God, we will one day live eternally in heaven as well. In essence, the one who has deceased is better off. They are at peace in the arms of the Lord. God brought your loved one to the firm resolve to leave this earth. Therefore, you must make the firm resolve to move forward with thanksgiving in your heart.

You may not be thankful that you will never see your loved one again on this earth but praise God that you will see them again one day. This thought did not bring much comfort in the beginning stages of my grief. The pain was too overwhelming, and I realized that when I do see my husband in heaven, we will not be husband and wife, but children of God. The reality remained that I had to live without my husband here on earth. I was now a widow, a woman living on earth alone without her husband by her side. This sorrow was too deep to express verbally. But as my faith began to take hold of my heart, even while grieving, I had to praise God for death. For it is through death that we will see God face to face. Death is the gateway to heaven and ultimate healing from the challenges we face in this life. Paul expresses this very eloquently in 2 Corinthians 5:1-8 (NKJV):

> For we know that if our earthly house, this tent, is destroyed, we have a building from God, a house not made with hands, eternal in the heavens. For in this we groan, earnestly desiring to be clothed with our habitation which is from heaven, if indeed, having been clothed, we shall not be found naked. For we who are in this tent groan, being burdened, not because we want to be unclothed, but further clothed, that mortality may be swallowed up by life. Now He who has prepared us for this very thing is God, who also has given us the Spirit

as a guarantee. So we are always confident, knowing that while we are at home in the body we are absent from the Lord. For we walk by faith, not by sight.

I discovered that the shock of losing your loved one takes time to sink in. This process is why I suggest that you must stay close to the Lord by whatever means necessary. To walk by faith and not by sight means to totally trust God. Our time in this earthly body is short for we are heavenly citizens. Jesus Christ is LORD and ruler. Our steps are ordered by God because we are the sheep of His pasture. We didn't make ourselves; God made us. Our home is in heaven. We are here to live out our purpose. The fact that our loved one passed away means that they fulfilled their purpose. So I am grateful that Raliegh filled his purpose. If it were not so, God would not have taken him home.

In case you are unsure of your loved one's eternal state, you must come to the calm resolve that they made personal choices while alive. You are not responsible for the choices your spouse made. We are all ultimately responsible for ourselves and the consequences of the choices we make. We must understand that our relationship with God is personal. However, we will never really know what happens in those final moments of life. Your loved one could have made a decision to surrender to God on the very threshold of death. At this point, there is nothing you can do about it other than to continue to give God thanks for life as we know it. You can mourn over the past, or choose to move forward and receive God's blessings of joy and peace, cleansing, and healing. You still have the opportunity to choose the happiness that God provides. The reality is that death provided a new life in eternity for the deceased, but it also provided an opportunity for a new life for those left behind. Take a look around and give thanks for what God has done. But also, take the time to give thanks for all of the many wonderful possibilities of your future.

I have heard some people say that they didn't have time to grieve over the loss of their loved one because of various responsibilities, so they take the time to work up sorrow and sadness over what could have, should have and would have been. They visit the cemetery every day, every week, every month. They constantly talk about the death event. Grant it, some issues should be dealt with to move forward. But is this God's way of grieving? At some point in your journey, the cure for overwhelming sorrow is to embrace opportunities to shift your thinking positively. Philippians 4:8 says: "And now, dear brothers and sisters, one final thing. Fix your thoughts on what is true, and honorable, and right, and pure, and lovely, and admirable. Think about things that are excellent and worthy of praise."

One day I decided to go on a thirty day fast and write only praises in my journal each day. Writing in my journal forced me to praise God intentionally for His blessings because I had to put it on paper. Each day was spent fixing my thoughts on all of the good things of the world. I couldn't deny the stress in my life at the time, but I chose not to dwell on that because I couldn't do anything about my circumstances. Some months down the road, I read this journal of praise. It was phenomenal. I was so blessed by what I read. It felt as if I was reading the words of another person. It became apparent to me at that moment that thoughts of praise overshadowed my grief. I was able to read later my journal pages of praise and thanksgiving on days when my sorrow felt overwhelming.

Being thankful are not just words on paper or praises from your lips, but it is an attitude that drives the very core of your being. Being thankful also means that peace comes from an eternal state of mind that permeates throughout your being. God has put eternity in the hearts of all of His children. As God's child, you must realize that you are just a stranger traveling through this land to your heavenly home. For that very reason, you must count your blessings and praise God that even though you lost your loved one, you haven't lost everything.

Although I was present when my husband passed, I gained a deeper reverence and worship for God. I recognized that I saw God at work as He took one of His children home. God is in complete control of life and death. I am humbled by this because I know that one day I must go down this same path. So as I think about my life and the fact that God is in control, I must give Him thanks not only for being alive but for my quality of life. I thank God that although I lost my husband, I didn't lose my mind. I didn't lose my soul. I didn't lose many of the things that he and I worked for. My children were still here. I still had a career. I still had other family and friends. I still had my relationship with God. Because of the many blessings, I could look around and thank God for the potential of living an even better-blessed life. I thank God for doors that will be opened, even when some doors are closed. I thank God that my heart was still strong enough to recognize that I needed to humble myself through this process of healing.

As you journal your way to a life of thanksgiving and praise, take the time to thank God for the gift of salvation that comes through the sacrifice and shed blood of His Son Jesus Christ. He died so that we might have an abundant life overflowing with His love, peace and blessings. The blood of Jesus Christ cleanses covers, heals, delivers, and gives those who trust in Him the strength and courage to move in a miraculous way through every traumatic situation.

Every good and perfect gift comes from God. You can thank God for the ability to do everything that you can do. Some people cannot do what you do, but God has favored you to be who you are and do what you do. God has created nature and beauty for you to behold. He has given you gifts and talents as an avenue to express that which is in your soul. God has given you intellect and the ability to think and reason. You can praise God for His love and his faithfulness, and for all of the things, He has already done. You can praise God for your healing. If you don't have peace yet, praise Him for it anyhow! It is surely on the way!

MOVING FORWARD

- ➢ Take a 21-day praise break. Start a journal and write about all of the things you are thankful for.
- ➢ Make a decision to pursue a dream or vision that has been lying dormant in your heart. Find out what it takes to make it happen and take one step at a time.
- ➢ Speak positive affirmations over yourself. Life is good. You are healed, happy and whole.
- ➢ Learn how to accept people for who they are. Be patient and kind.
- ➢ Rebuke the fear of starting a new relationship, give love another chance. If it doesn't turn into marriage, praise God for the companionship. It all works together for good.
- ➢ Make new friends. Create new memories.
- ➢ Don't focus on your weaknesses, but celebrate what makes you strong.

- It's not arrogant to toot your own horn, learn to give thanks for what God has put in you!
- As you change your outlook on life, also change your outlook on death. God created both.
- You only have one life to live. Let go of the pain and give yourself permission to live life to its fullest.

THE SUPPORT TEAM

- Deal with your thoughts about death so that you can speak positively to the one you are encouraging.
- Help guide the conversation on how life is different and not on life was with the deceased. Accepting that life is different is part of the process of gradually letting go.
- Help the one grieving to list positive ways that life is different.
- Avoid making assumptions based on the outward appearance of the situation.
- Offer support and encourage the one grieving to make new relationships.

FURTHER REFLECTION:

Don't be afraid to make new friends and do new things. Positively embrace that life will never be the same. Look for new opportunities. Read the following scriptures and write your reflections: Ecclesiastes 4:7-12, Ezekiel 1:12, Job 17:9,1 Corinthians 2:9

8

MOURNING OR HAPPINESS…
You Choose

> "Most people are about as happy as they
> make up their minds to be."
> ~Abraham Lincoln

> So I concluded there is nothing better than to be
> happy and enjoy ourselves as long as we can. And
> people should eat and drink and enjoy the fruits
> of their labor, for these are gifts from God.
> ~Ecclesiastes 3:12-13(NLT)

What is happiness anyway? According to Webster's dictionary, happiness is defined as: "a state of well-being and contentment, joy or a pleasurable or satisfying experience, good fortune or prosperity." We may not all agree on how to achieve happiness. Nevertheless, I believe that we can agree on the premise that everyone wants to be happy, whether they verbalize it or not. It's human nature. I must admit that I share the same view as Abraham Lincoln's statement that, "Most people are as happy as they make up their minds to be." If you want to be happy, then you will find happiness even in the midst of trials and tribulations. You will intentionally steer your mind toward happy thoughts, happy things, and happy people. You will seek out the positive and the good, even when bad things are happening.

You may wonder if it is possible to achieve a state of contentment and well-being after living through the traumatic experience of pain and grief. The answer is, yes you can. I have heard many people say that in time, things will get better. You will feel better about life. You will heal. As the saying goes, "time heals all wounds." However, I have discovered, that it is not necessarily time alone that heals all wounds, but it is your state of mind and the decision to move forward from this event that brings about full healing. A small cut, if left alone can heal by itself if the body is healthy and you already possess good health habits. But that same small cut can become a large infected wound if left alone and the body itself is not in good health. For example, a person with the disease of diabetes doesn't heal as easily from wounds. Additionally, bad habits increase the risk of infection. I believe this same principle is at work when it comes to peace and happiness.

First of all, there is the satisfaction that comes from following your passion and living in the will of God. God pours into your soul an inward peace and joy that is infused supernaturally into your very being. As I mentioned previously, the path to purpose includes pain and loss. The key to overcoming pain to achieve happiness is to shift the focus from grief to positive expectations of life and the people built on the foundation of faith for God's perfect plan to manifest in you.

Who are you? What are you doing now? How are you doing it? Where are you going in life? How will you get there? What is your passion? What and who in your life brings you joy and fulfillment? What makes one happy will not necessarily make another happy. Therefore, you must learn to be content and become comfortable with who you are and where you are at this particular point in time. You must believe God for healing, and trust the fact that He is able and willing to heal. It is imperative that you cooperate with this healing by making the decision to experience joy and happiness in your life again. Look for it with great anticipation. Feeling secure in who God created you to be while pursuing Him will bring satisfaction to your life. Nonetheless, I believe that there is absolutely nothing wrong with incorporating things into your life that make you happy.

LEARN TO ENJOY LIFE

Let me remind you of a very real truth, YOU ARE STILL ALIVE! You have been left here on this earth for a reason and a season. So you might as well learn to laugh and enjoy life. As a matter of fact, laughing is good for the soul. Proverbs 17:22 says; "A cheerful heart is good medicine, but a broken spirit saps a person's strength." I know from experience that this scripture is right on point. Crying all night and grieving all day wears you out. Sleepless nights drain your energy level. Grieving is stressful and causes other physical ailments. There is a song by Pharrell Williams entitled "Happy." Every time I hear that song, I smile. I love seeing the dancing and singing in the video because of all of the joy and happiness it exudes. Because of its positive effect, this song has become viral. A cheerful heart is contagious and good for your soul. People need and desire happiness. Would you rather cry or smile? You choose! In the midst of my journey of healing, God inspired me to look around and appreciate my life, the people in it and all of life's possibilities. I made a choice!

The pursuit of being the best you can be physically is as critical as the journey to emotional wellness. It is very easy to become consumed by all of the responsibilities of making adjustments to a new life that you neglect your health and well-being. It is very crucial to adopt and maintain good health habits of rest, diet and exercise so that you will have the physical energy to enjoy your life. I found it very beneficial to begin to walk outdoors enjoying nature instead of the treadmill. Going to the gym with all of the hustle and bustle of people working out motivated me to pursue a healthy lifestyle. Subsequently, the pursuit of good health gave me something else positive and productive to channel your energy.

One of the other pursuits I love is traveling to see new places and experience new things. I went to the beach on vacation by myself about a year after becoming widowed and loved it. One person asked me if I was going to meet someone because they couldn't believe I would just get up and do that alone. My reply was that I do not have a mate so I would have to learn to enjoy and explore life without a mate. Otherwise, I would always be afraid to venture out alone. I would be stuck in the house doing the same old thing! Nevertheless, I had a fantastic time. Every day was a new adventure. I planned out the sights I would see each day and enjoyed every minute. I didn't feel alone because I was motivated and thankful to God by the fact that this vacation brought so much pleasure after experiencing so much pain. Aside from that, I have a highly curious and adventuresome nature. I have to include activities in my life that satisfy this God-given trait in my personality.

I have taken other vacations alone and traveled to see and meet friends and family. My first international trip was to Seoul, Korea to visit a friend. We taught together many years ago. She saw that I was retiring and invited me to experience something life on another level. I love her for nudging me in that direction. This exerience was also very crucial to me moving forward and finding purpose in my pain. I have done missions in Liberia, West Africa, in which we are now connected to a network of churches with a school named in my honor. This international relationship is very rewarding. My girlfriends from college and I periodically take trips just to get away. I have a bucket list of places that I have never been but intend to visit. When convenient, I take advantage of every opportunity that presents itself for me to travel. Meeting people of various cultures and seeing the vast canvas of God's creation gives meaning, beauty, and purpose to live.

There are other activities and hobbies I enjoy that have added meaning and purpose to my life. Reading is one. Reading an excellent book with a great story or positive affirmations can be very therapeutic. Developing a gift or talent makes life meaningful and purposeful. My special gift is music, and the ability to play the piano and sing. There were times when I would get up in the middle of the night and play the piano. Music is very therapeutic and a great stress reliever. Listening to music also connects me spiritually to my Maker. I feel peace and tranquility as heart and mind become engulfed in the rhythms, melodies, and instrumentation. God gave me this gift so it stands to reason that I would connect with Him as He pours into me through this gift.

There are simple things in life that can lift your spirit. It may not be music but activities such as going to the movies, viewing a parade, eating ice cream, walking through the park, going to visit a museum, and all of the other readily available activities offered right before your eyes. Having a conversation with great people who stimulate your intellect, creativity and passions can do wonders! Enjoyable activities can fill your heart with love and appreciation for life. You will find yourself looking forward to waking up every day and striking out on a new adventure when you allow yourself to shift out of the pain mode to the purpose mode. There is a whole world waiting to be discovered by you. Pick up a calendar and make a plan to explore. You can't afford to wait on someone else to make it happen; you have to make it happen.

One other thing I learned through this challenging season of grief was how to appreciate the people God has placed in my life. It is a waste of time to linger on the ailments of life and petty grievances. I have never been one to hold a grudge or harbor offenses. Losing someone so close and dear to me suddenly, caused me to be more determined than ever to guard my heart against holding grudges. An unforgiving spirit causes much grief and sorrow in the average person. You would not want to compound the pain of losing a loved one with harbored bitter feelings of unforgiveness.

As you look around and consider the brevity of life, you will find that much of what causes division and conflict between people is irrelevant to the meaning and purpose of life. Besides, practicing love and forgiveness as Jesus did brings a sense of divine peace and joy to your soul. The feeling of stability and security from this attitude opens the door to a happy life that cannot be shaken. Keeping life simple and thanking God for the people, places, and things right before your eyes cultivate happiness like a watered garden. I believe this honors the life of your deceased loved one.

Some people are in your life for a season and others that are there for a lifetime. However, I have learned that even the most unlovable person you encounter has a purpose in your life. They may cause stress and frustration, but you must trust that all things will work out for your good. God will make all things beautiful in its time. God has given you a life to live and enjoy – even through the trials and tribulations – the toils and snares, God has reserved the special gift of happiness that He pours out with much grace to those who love and trust Him. Life is too short, as they say, to spend all of your days grieving and looking back.

KING SOLOMON AND THE TRUE MEANING OF LIFE

Have you ever noticed that there are many unhappy people in the world? People pursue happiness in healthy and unhealthy ways. The challenge we face is that which makes us happy today, may not work tomorrow. King Solomon says in Ecclesiastes 2:22-23, "For what has man for all his labor, and for the striving of his heart with which he has toiled under the sun? For all his days are sorrowful, and his work burdensome; even in the night his heart takes no rest. This also is vanity." The word vanity in this scripture indicates the concept of pointlessness, meaninglessness—like trying to chase the wind or grab a hold of a rainbow.

When people see life as pointless, they sometimes search for happiness in negative ways. Therefore, what they are experiencing is a momentary thrill, but not true happiness. Let me encourage you not to fall into that trap. As you move through the grief process, make sure you do not choose negative behavior such as drugs and alcohol, partying, uncontrolled spending, and bad relationships. Unhealthy choices will only magnify your grief and derail your road to happiness.

You will find that moving from pain to healing and on to the strengthening process, happiness will come as you submit to God's purpose in your life. It's easier than fighting to making something happen that God did not intend. Living on purpose brings peace and happiness. Furthermore, the type of happiness we should be seeking is the joy and happiness that God gives, which is lasting and fulfilling. You may feel that the thrill is gone; the happiness is gone and was taken away by the loss of your mate. But God will help you find new meaning in life, which will bring lasting happiness.

King Solomon seems to have come to the resolve that in spite of all of the foolishness, folly, vanity and labor of life, he would live a life of rejoicing in the goodness of God. He was known as the richest, wisest, and most powerful man of his time. He had 700 concubines and many treasures. He built a lavish temple along with a lavish palace. His writings in the book of Ecclesiastes reflect his search for the meaning of life in the midst of all of the struggles that he encountered. Because of the wisdom God bestowed upon him, he had very keen insight into the activities of man and his relationship with God. Men would have to toil day in and day out to live a happy and prosperous life. In the midst of these days of toil and labor were seasons of pain and grief. However, he expounds throughout the book that God's purpose prevails through it all. He reaches the conclusion that the meaning of life could only be found in the gift of the Almighty God who is sovereign and rules over everything in the earth.

Solomon was also distressed by activities of people who foolishly lived as if there was no God or no tomorrow. He stated in Ecclesiastes 3:11-13:

> God has made everything beautiful for its own time. He has planted eternity in the human heart, but even so, people cannot see the whole scope of God's work from

> beginning to end. So I concluded there is nothing better
> than to be happy and enjoy ourselves as long as we can.
> And people should eat and drink and enjoy the fruits of
> their labor, for these are gifts from God.

Solomon encourages the reader to view life through the lens of the Divine perspective. There is a bigger picture in which God is working everything in the earth according to His eternal plan for all of His creation. Throughout the book of Ecclesiastes, Solomon examines all of man's activities in life, his work, his relationships, the sorrows and the joys of life. But he states over and over in some form or another that all of man's activities are meaningless against the backdrop of God's plans from the beginning of time until the end. Your life and the painful trauma that you experienced is just one piece of the puzzle in the big scheme of things. No one can understand how God works, but you must rest assured that every person will die one day. You must trust God in the meantime.

Your loved one might have preceded you in death, but you will also die one day. That's why Solomon says in Ecclesiastes 8:15: "So I recommend having fun because there is nothing better for people in this world than to eat, drink, and enjoy life. That way they will experience some happiness along with all the hard work God gives them under the sun." The level of happiness that Solomon is describing comes from one's relationship with God. No matter what you do to make yourself happy, Solomon learned that although he practically had everything he could ever dream of, this did not bring him happiness. He also says in Ecclesiastes 12:13; "Here now is my final conclusion: Fear God and obey his commands, for this is everyone's duty." In essence, this is the foundation of lasting happiness.

THE OIL OF JOY

True happiness proceeds from the spirit of joy that abides deep down in the soul. Joy can be described as the quality of the state of mind which finds delight, pleasure, and satisfaction in life. Lasting joy comes from learning to be content. It's alright to pursue dreams and experiences in life that bring joy and happiness. It is a blessing to be around positive and cheerful people. However, make sure you do not lose sight of the fact that true happiness is not dependent on external things, people, or the places you go. True happiness comes from within, flowing from the spirit of joy. Contentment flows from living a life of praise and worship to God Almighty for all of his many blessings. Your life could be much worse.

This deep abiding joy is a gift of God which comes through Jesus Christ and by the Holy Spirit. Joy is not just a happy feeling but is the steady and constant calm assurance that things will work out for good. This joy flows from the presence of God and permeates your countenance and outlook on life. This joy expects the best and wants the best. It will give you the strength and courage to make the necessary adjustments to move forward. This joy also comes from a deep abiding trust that God wants the best for you, no matter what you may be facing at the moment.

The question is, "How do you choose happiness and an attitude of gratitude when the pain is so overwhelming?" The answer is simply to make a deliberate and intentional decision to shift your perspective and then do what it takes to make it happen. The mind is very powerful. Many people don't make the choice to be happy because they don't know that happiness exists. Furthermore, many people choose to continue to mourn because they think that mourning honors the deceased. They are afraid that if they stop grieving, they are permanently letting go of their loved one. But is this not what is needed to move forward? There is no need to feel guilty for moving forward. Let me say again – remember that you are still alive! Shedding your garments of mourning reflect your faith in God and positive outlook of your faith that whether in life or death, we all still belong to God. He will never leave nor forsake His children in life or death.

The custom of mourners during Bible times was to wear sackcloth and put ashes on their heads and face to publicly indicate their deep sorrow. They would not oil or anoint their heads (we might identify this custom in modern times as putting on lotion, makeup, perfumes, jewelry, and so on.), but would instead crown themselves with ashes. Their mourning was characterized by the spirit of heaviness, which is translated into fainthearted, feeble or weak. However, according to Isaiah 61:3, Jesus was anointed to…

> "…console those who mourn in Zion,
> To give them beauty for ashes,

> The oil of joy for mourning,
> The garment of praise for the spirit of heaviness;
> That they may be called trees of righteousness,
> The planting of the LORD, that He may be glorified."

In this scripture, the prophet Isaiah foretells the ministry of Jesus Christ. The principal message is that through faith in Jesus Christ, all will be healed from grief because God sent His only begotten Son to earth to give us eternal life through salvation, which includes many promises. It describes those mourning as taking off their mourning clothes and putting on garments of praise. As a result, they would shed all symbols of grief and exhibit praise to God for His anointing of deliverance from all sorrow and oppression. They would appear as trees or oaks of righteousness, which symbolized strength, hope and steadfastness because of their relationship with Him. The people around them would witness their strength, resilience and constant praise and service to God Almighty, and draw to Him.

Beloved, God has already prepared the solution for healing from grief. It is through our belief in Jesus Christ. To move forward, we must receive this gift promised to all of those who trust in God. God will anoint all those who mourn with the oil of joy and beauty for ashes.

THE BEST IS YET TO COME

Do you believe it? If so, embrace the best and move forward. The best is yet to come! There is a saying that beauty lies in the eyes of the beholder. I believe the same is true about life. Do you view your future through the lens of pain and disappointment, or do you see life through the prism of positive expectations of blessings, peace and prosperity? If you seek to uncover the worst, you will see the worst and live beneath the beautiful experiences this life has to offer. If you look for the best, you will see and live the best. You can't embrace the best if all you think about is the worst. Likewise, if you expect the worse in the people God has placed in your life, you will see the worse. I believe that the experience of losing a loved one should cause one to appreciate better the best in others, and value others for who they are.

It is sometimes difficult to expect the best when the world surrounds us with negatiity. Our culture seems to thrive on pessimism and the misfortune of others. People who kill, steal and destroy others in one form or another dominate the news. Does this sound familiar? Jesus said to the disciples in John 10:10: "The thief comes only to steal and kill and destroy; I have come that they may have life, and have it to the full." In other words, don't let grief and sorrow, pessimism and negativity bitterness, unforgiveness, self-pity, and selfishness steal your joy. It may be difficult to believe in the midst of pain and disappointment. However, you have the choice to receive by faith that the season of mourning and sorrow is only a temporary state.

As I pen the last few pages of this book, I am grateful to God for giving me this perfect illustration. Today, my children and I are in National Harbor, Maryland at Christmas on the Potomac to celebrate this season and to welcome a new addition to our family. I mentioned in an earlier chapter that moving forward will eventually require creating new memories and new experiences. Moving forward also demands that we change our expectations of the effects of certain family events. Life is different. You shared some good times with your deceased loved one, but life can and will get better if you let it.

Traditionally, we would be at home, which would usually lead to a family time of reflection of the past and present. Being away from home on Christmas day is different, but it is so nice and relaxing! I decided to take a walk on the river to enjoy the scenery and warm weather as I also meditate on how to bring this last chapter to a close. While standing on the dock, I noticed the thick fog on the river. Suddenly I heard very clearly an audible voice impress in my spirit that life will not always be a fog.

For many people, grief and loss lead to much uncertainty. Other losses grieve us such as job loss, divorce, finances, friends and the death of other close relationships. Visions of the future appear as thick as the fog I just witnessed on the river. It's hard to imagine that your future will be brighter when you are dealing with doubt and fear. It is also difficult to embrace more glorious future if you demand answers for all of your questions, and that your expectations come to pass. I discovered that the secret to joy and happiness as you move forward is to release your foggy interpretation of how life should be. You must also release the foggy understanding of the world around you and embrace the possibilities of life. God has already fashioned your days and opened the doors of opportunity. The only way to walk through those doors and reset your life is to look forward in anticipation that the fog will dissipate. It always does! Life will become clearer and your days will become brighter.

How do you deal with the foggy times of your life? A good biblical illustration of a foggy time in life can found in the book of Jeremiah, a prophet called by God to deliver the message of warning and judgment to the children of Israel. They would be captured and sent to the foreign land of Babylon for 70 years. Jerusalem would be destroyed, homes would be burned, and the temple would be desecrated. Loved ones would die during the invasion while others would be deported to Babylon as slaves. God allowed this trial for a particular reason, but it had a set time to begin and a set time to end. In Jeremiah 29, the people were encouraged to make the best of their captivity. They were to buy homes, plant fields, develop their businesses, marry and have children while seeking the peace of the city. Although they did not want to live in the foreign land, they were to help make the city prosperous so that they could benefit from its prosperity. However, the motivation for making the best of their circumstances is described best in verses 10-11:

> For thus says the LORD: After seventy years are completed at Babylon, I will visit you and perform My good word toward you, and cause you to return to this place. For I know the thoughts that I think toward you, says the LORD, thoughts of peace and not of evil, to give you a future and a hope.

These verses and the ones that follow reassure God's chosen people that in spite of trauma and tragedy, God's agenda for the future was that of restoration. They would suffer only for a season, but as they called on God in prayer, He would comfort them with His presence. According to God's agenda, the future held peace and prosperity. They were to rejoice with hope and patiently wait on God to move because their expected end was good. He promised to lead them back to their homeland, but it would be a new beginning. Life would never be the same. They would be a new nation because their perspective on life would change in light of their tragic experience. But God promised to change their weeping into dancing, their sorrow into joy and their loss into gain. Yes indeed, the best was yet to come because God was working behind the scenes. However, this new season had an appointed time to come to pass. It had already taken place in the mind of God, but the new season had yet to become a physical reality. The people were not to live in fear and dread, but with positive expectation.

I would be remiss if I didn't also mention the life of Ruth, the most famous widow in the Bible. In fact, there is a whole book in the Bible named Ruth containing principles and illustrations of God's intention to give the best to His chosen ones. The main characters are Ruth, who was from Moab and her mother-in-law Naomi, who was an Israelite.

In summary, Naomi was living in Moab with her husband and two sons. They migrated there as a result of the famine in Jerusalem. Naomi's two sons married wives from Moab. Eventually, Naomi's husband dies, and then her two sons. Being a widow in Bible days was very detrimental being that the women depended on their fathers, husbands, sons, or other male family members for livelihood. After losing her husband and then her sons, Naomi became bitter and insisted on changing her name to Mara. She decides to go back home to her kinsmen because she had lost everything. Her grief was so intense that she had given up hope of a better life.

Ruth chose to follow her mother-in-law to Jerusalem and leave her kinsmen in Moab. Leaving her homeland and her famiy a big leap of faith. Although Naomi encouraged Ruth to stay in Moab, she decided that Naomi's God would be her God. She optimistically made a significant change in her life to ensure that her better days were yet to come. In short, she moves to Jerusalem, meets Boaz, who becomes her Kinsman Redeemer. They gave birth to a son named Obed, who incidentally became the joy of Naomi's life, who was the ancestor of King David and Jesus Christ. Ruth is one of four women mentioned in the genealogy of Jesus Christ (Matthew 1:5, 16).

However, she had to overcome many obstacles before receiving this wonderful gift of a husband and a child. For one, Ruth was from Moab and had no means to support herself, whose people were considered repulsive enemies of the Jews. Furthermore, she and Boaz had to deal with the laws

Moving Forward: Finding Purpose in Your Pain

and elders of Jerusalem before they could become engaged. But in spite of the dark days and the many obstacles, God was working behind the scenes to fulfill His ultimate plan of salvation through Jesus Christ. Ruth stepped out on faith and hope in God, and eventually, He blessed her to remarry and give birth.

I don't know where you are in your journey through pain to living out purpose, but I encourage you to hold on to the precious promise that your best is yet to come and keep moving forward. Just as God promised restoration to the children of Israel in the book of Jeremiah, and the life of Ruth, God's plans for you are good for every area of your life. You may not be able to see it, but you must walk by faith and not by sight believing that He is working things out. Psalm 34:8 says: "O taste and see that the Lord is good. Blessed is the man who trusts in Him." To taste means to ingest and saturate your inner being with the resolve to believe that God intends to bless your life. It means to move forward regardless of discouragement, disappointment, and dark days. Think it, believe it, live it, and say to the masses that the Lord God is good and that your best days are being worked out. You must trust and give God praise for unseen blessings and open doors. Grief won't last forever. Your life won't be turned upside down indefinitely. There is a rainbow at the end of this storm.

Someone asked me the other day, "What lessons am I supposed to learn from all of the losses in my life?" As I reflect on my experience, the lessons I have learned from working through the pain and the foggy days to moving forward and finding purpose in my pain are explained throughout this book. But my closing thoughts are that:

- ➢ God is in charge of death and life. Grieving will not change what has already occurred, so train your mind and heart to look forward by seeking God's plan. Everyone has to die.
- ➢ Your loved one became one with the plan of God and came to a resolve to leave this earth to be with the Lord. Therefore, you must come to the resolve to stay here and enjoy life as you fulfill your purpose.
- ➢ There are much worse things that could happen in life. Therefore, praise God and claim the best.
- ➢ Lastly, moving forward means to….

Live life simply, on purpose, in purpose and with purpose,
Laugh as much as you can, when and with whom you can,
Love unconditionally, accepting people for who they are.
The Best is yet to come!
Embrace your future on purpose and move forward.

MOVING FORWARD

- Try to find meaning in the trauma you have experienced – pray – meditate – exercise and adopt an exercise regimen – be the best you. Explore a new look or new style.
- Don't beat yourself up for what you think you could have, should have and should not have done – look forward, think forward, make decisions that will move you forward.
- Make a decision today to choose happiness over mourning. This decision will drive your actions and activities to make choices that yield positive results with positive people.
- Trust solely in God's care, protection, provisions, presence, comfort, love, peace, grace and mercy. His plans for you are great.
- Identify your support group so that you have someone to talk to and laugh with when needed. If you don't think you have that group right now, then get out make new friends. Everybody needs somebody at some point in life.
- Do what makes you happy, even if it makes others uncomfortable. If it's okay with you and God, everyone else will get over it.

THE SUPPORT TEAM

- The best advice I can give to you at this stage of the game is that you may not always agree with the decisions made by the one grieving, but you should support them if this decision brings peace and comfort to their life.
- If the decision is totally off course morally, irrationally, illegally, or anything that can be harmful or detrimental to the person you are encouraging, then you should take the actions necessary to assist

this person in coming to their senses. Don't just pray for them, but pray with them. There is power in prayer.
- ➢ Also, you can benefit as well from having a merry heart. Don't just cry together, but laugh together. Talk about the good things in life. There is so much to be thankful for. God has made all things beautiful in His time!

FURTHER REFLECTION

Life is too short to grieve for the rest of your days on earth. Praise God for your life, by living it to the fullest. Read the following scriptures and record your reflections: Ruth 1-4, Psalms 90:12, James 1:2-6, Psalm 30:1-5.

ABOUT THE AUTHOR

A mother, preacher, teacher, musician, singer, friend and mentor are words that many use to describe her. However, born-again, spirit-filled, a friend and lover of God are words that may best describe this vessel of God. Through her ministry of teaching and preaching, many have received healing, deliverance, and illumination into the Word, Wisdom, and Will of God. Her greatest passion is to encourage, equip and empower others to fulfill their divine purpose.

She presently serves as the Senior Pastor of the Greenhill Church and Christian Outreach Ministries and CEO of The Greenhill Human Development Corporation. She was licensed in 1996 as a Minister of the Gospel, and later ordained in 1999. In addition to serving as Pastor, her ministry extends to preaching and teaching for conferences, revivals and other church / Christian related events, as well as motivational speaking for community events and organizations. In June 2014, she was invited to speak as the first international speaker for the St. Paul Church of Christ, a network of 23 churches in Liberia, West Africa. As a result, the Angela Roberts Jones Elementary School located in Grand Bassa County, Liberia, a school established by these churches was named in her honor. Subsequently, she has established and serves as General Overseer of the Liberia I Care Mission /Kingdom Expansion International Ministries to provide missions to these schools and churches in Liberia.

A native of Sylvania, Georgia, she is a magna-cum-laude graduate of Fisk University of Nashville, TN where she received a B.S. in Music Education. She considers traveling as a member of the well renowned Jubilee Singers as one of her most rewarding and honorable experiences while at Fisk. She also holds a Master of Music Degree from Southern Illinois University, and a M. A. in Theological Studies from Liberty University. In addition, she is a Retired Educator and author of African American History Month Daily Devotionals 2014. She resides in Clarksville, TN where she is actively involved in serving her community in several organizations and boards.

You may learn more about her at: www.arjonesministries.com

Printed in the United States
By Bookmasters